Occupy Peace Now

Restore Peace, Liberty, Honesty, Rule of Law, Sound Money, and the Constitution. End Empire-USA

Author: David Redick

The author gratefully acknowledges permission to reprint excerpts from the books of leading authors. Text and data are also included from think-tanks, blogs, and the government. All are attributed by showing the web site of the source adjacent to the display of the text or data. When not expressly granted, permission is based on Fair Use laws.
This book is intended to support and promote 'OccupyPeace' (OccupyPeace.us), which is a project of the Trends Research Institute, Inc. (TrendsResearch.com), Gerald Celente, Founder and Director. This book is not authorized by the Institute, so while it intends to represent the authors' understanding the goals of the project, the books' content is soley the responsibility of the author.

Edition	Date	Pages
1	October 15, 2015	160

Published by the 'Forward USA Foundation'.
ISBN-13: 978-1517556679
ISBN-10: 1517556678

Printed in the United States of America by createspace.com. This book, and others by Dave, can be purchased from major book sellers such as Amazon.com.

This book is dedicated to the U.S. citizens who are aware and concerned about the many illegal, immoral and counterproductive acts of our government, which have caused our decline into less Peace, Liberty, Prosperity, and Justice in the USA. We are now approaching a crash of our economy and culture, and the author hopes this book will help others to 'wake up' and join the www.OccupyPeace.us project to help end the damage and start the recovery.

****

These wise words, written long ago by an unknown author, offer support to our work for www.OccupyPeace.us.

'The Founding Fathers were not career politicians. They were the outlaws, the angry extremists, who refused to quietly submit to an elite political establishments' oppression over their lives.
Never forget that!

"Government is not reason; it is not eloquence; it is force. Like fire, it is a dangerous servant and a fearful master.",   George Washington

'Government is not the solution to our problems, it is the problem.' by Ronal Reagan at his first inaugural, Jan-1981.

Sen. Robert Taft said; "The purpose of our foreign policy must be to protect the liberty of the people of the United States."

Sen. Jack Kemp said; "There are no limits to our future if we don't put limits on our people. It is empirically true and historically convincing that with lower rates of taxation on labor, capital, and the factors of production, you will get a bigger economy.";

Paul Craig Roberts, PhD. (PaulCraigRoberts.org) wrote: "Washington's argument is that unless Americans accept the most complete police-state in history, they will not be safe. Consequently, today no American is safe from his own government."

Gerald Celente (TrendsResearch.com) wrote; "Until the USA gives up taking sides, in foreign internal conflicts, policing the world, and using its power to 'spread democracy', 'open markets', and protect special interests in the name of our national interests, the terrorism trend will continue."

"When the government fears the People, that is Liberty. When the People fear the Government, that is tyranny." - Thomas Jefferson

Richard Ebeling, PhD., Sep-2015; Critics of capitalism constantly insist on the "failure" of the free market, from the news pundits to the leftist leaders of political parties. Yet, in fact, the asserted "failures" of capitalism are really the inevitable results of the interventionist-welfare state, and the close relationships between government and special interest groups popularly called "crony capitalism.

Contents

Part 1:

Part 2:

****

Part 1
Introduction

War and domestic unrest and riots are expensive and the opposite of peace. This book offers a plan to achieve sustainable Peace, Liberty, and Prosperity, by ending;
1) The wars we start, and join, to support our immoral and failed goals of expanding Empire-USA, and acting as the world's policeman and boss, and
2) Our expensive and counterproductive domestic regulations, welfare programs, and police-state policies.

Foreign Wars and Empire
The USA has been seeking expansion of its land and power since the failed 'War of 1812'. We added vast lands to make our current southwest by starting the 'Mexican-American War', sought power and land in the Pacific with the 'Spanish-American War', and emerged from World War 1 as a leader, and from WW2 as a rich superpower. The Korean and Vietnam wars were a loss in both the military and moral sense. Of course the '9/11' tragedy started the endless 'War on Terror' that is still growing. The Federal government uses it to justify murder or invasion any person and any place! There is ample evidence that the 9/11 buildings fell due to explosive demolition (not airplane crashes), and was planned by the Bush Gang in DC to give them a 'Pearl Harbor' type event to justify wars, etc. for their political (control the world under Empire-USA, defend Israel, etc.), and economic (mostly oil) goals.
Note that all of the wars since the 1776 Revolution were started on lies by the President, and were for gaining wealth and power (economic and political goals), not for homeland defense! (more in Appendix 1, p. 136)

Domestic Welfare and Police
Since the start of FDR's social and business welfare programs in 1933, the government (both Federal and most States) has been acting as Nanny to the citizens and

industry with various expensive welfare, subsidies, and special privilege programs that reduce incentive to; 1) use personal responsibility, 2) manage your life to avoid or solve your own problems (health, career, family, etc.), and 3) improve your economic worth for better pay. Private charity is suggested for those people with disabilities that hinder their growth, but zero subsidies and legal privileges (tariffs, monopolies, etc.) for business.

This trend of anger and violence has allowed the local and federal government to adopt use of more deadly equipment ('militarized police'), and aggressive attitudes and conduct. The result is that the USA has become a police-state that reduces peace, and promotes violence.

Spending and Debt

Wars, Empires, and Welfare are expensive, and this book will discuss how our present, but declining, status as issuer of the world's primary reserve currency allows us to create new money (and borrow more) to pay for our present warfare- welfare oriented government.

We were spending our 'gold-backed' U.S. Dollar (USD) to extremes after WW2 (LBJ called it 'guns and butter') until Nixon ended redemption of paper money for gold in 1971, because we were running out of gold. All other countries also ended redemption, and the world started its carefree practice of spending more than they could afford to repay. The fiasco bankruptcies of Mexico, Argentina, Greece, and others since the 1990's are examples. Because it was issued by the world's largest economy, the new fiat (value is declared by issuer, not the free market) USD retained its status as the world's primary reserve currency (banks hold it as reserve for transactions, and any Seller will accept it). This has allowed us to pay our bills with newly created USD, and we have done it to extreme since 1971! The two primary negative effects have been; 1) The purchasing power of the USD declined due to 'monetary inflation' and prices increased due to the resultant 'price inflation' (by 10 times for most things since 1971), and 2) we became a 'consumer nation' and imported to excess, paid for with new money. This also caused jobs and factories to be sent overseas to further reduce costs, and thus jobs and technology were reduced (or gone) in the USA! **This can only be done by the nation which issues the world's primary reserve currency**, and pays with an unlimited supply of' new' money. The solution is commodity money (see Private Gold Standard p. 153) which limits excessive spending on imports (or you run out, or the foreign exchange rate soars!). We also borrowed to pay for our excess spending on wars abroad for empire, and consumption at home, causing our national debt to reach an unpayable, $18 trillion (Table 1)

A further problem is the concentration of power and money with the Federal government. This shift of power from the States to DC has grown our federal servant into a monster!

Since '9/11', we have increased our wars in the Mideast. These are for oil, and power, and some for the defense of Israel, and are destroying our morals, culture and economy! Our former 'allies' (fellow invaders and bombers) are now sometimes refusing to join our invasions (they need and fear us less). Thus, we are getting weak in many ways, and can be damaged physically or economically by despots at home, or by wealthy nations, probably led by Russia or China.

Citizens of the USA now face the same challenges and problems that our Founders did: repressive, corrupt, and excessive government. **We must stop the damage caused by Obama, future presidents, and the willing dupes in Congress, by replacing their unconstitutional schemes with my sustainable plan to 'Restore Peace and Prosperity' shown in Chapter 4!** The corruption of vote-seeking elected officials is an old problem. The Roman Empire is a good example. The USA has a growing percentage of Socialists, Liberals, Progressives, and Fascists who say the government should 'manage' almost everything at home, and 'lead and help the world' (the latter attracts Conservatives too, as a 'police' function). Now they have statist President Obama to lead them (see Fascism, Socialism, and Statist in the Glossary). I grant that many of the citizens who call themselves Liberals, and Progressives ('socialist' has lost favor due to its failures) may have good intentions to help 'the people and workers', and serve the 'common good'. The problem is that their projects do more harm than good (if all the side effects are counted) and the 'Caring Progressives' use immoral 'forced charity' fund-raising via taxation which I call 'gang theft by vote'! As discussed in Chapter 4, item 2 'Core Principle' things that are immoral if done by people, are just as immoral if done by the government. A 'good cause' does not justify fund-raising by gang theft. I recommend private charity to help others. Private fund raising is more work, but it is honest. Liberals who want to assist others financially should make a donation, volunteer to work, or start a new charity.

This book discusses how the USA got into its present economic, legal, and ethical mess, and presents a comprehensive, integrated plan on how to recover. History and logic support how the limited government, free-market approach will bring more Peace, liberty, prosperity, justice, and ethics for all.

For updates, to make a donation, or to read about other topics, visit the web site **OccupyPeace.us,** a project of' Trends Research Institute, Inc. (TrendsResearch.com), Gerald Celente, Founder and Director.

Thanks for your interest and support. See my biography at p. 156. You can contact me at RedickD@aol.com.

Best regards, Dave Redick

Chapter 1

USA Status: Economics and Politics

Chapter 4 of this book presents a comprehensive, integrated, plan on how to '**Restore Peace and Prosperity'.** It will give all citizens more Peace, Liberty and Justice, and open a choice of paths for all citizens to earn more Prosperity. It discusses the cause-and-effect correlation between: 1. Government violation of our rights and the Constitution, and 2. The corruption (illegal acts) and abuses (improper use of authority), and economic collapse we see around us in the USA, and worldwide.

As you read this book you will notice that I am angry at our 'leaders' and how they and their friends profit from the Illegal and abusive conduct of our government. I find that most political crooks (when caught) use mild, evasive, terms such as 'misspoke', 'misstep' or 'troubling' to describe what are in fact their overt, planned, lies, fraud, and theft, etc., not accidents, or mistakes, as 'mis' implies. We should make these scoundrels apologize, punish them (fines, loss of job, prison?), and keep our eyes on them to detect future misconduct. Strong talk? You bet; we are far past the time of acting 'nice' to the smiling, devious, self-serving, career-centered crooks who use the government to rob and abuse us from DC and elsewhere. Complacent citizens deserve the abuse they tolerate, good and hard! The opposite of complacency is activism. If you like the ideas in this book, DO SOMETHING!, such as be an active member of **www.OccupyPeace.us,** be a candidate for local or national office, write letters of complaint and suggestion to government officials, etc. This book pulls no punches, and goes to the heart of our social and economic problems, and how to solve them.

On the economic front, excessive spending and debt by both the people and government have placed our nation on the brink of economic collapse. Under 'normal' financial conditions, the people and government would run out of money and stop spending, but as discussed below and in Chapter 3, the US Dollar is the world's primary reserve currency (all Sellers and Lenders will accept and hold them) so we alone can create paper and digital dollars out of thin-air to pay our bills. The Bush-Obama style bailout and stimulus plans only prolong the pain by engaging in more spending and debt to save a corrupt and unsustainable system (often led by their friends and campaign donors) that should instead be reformed and replaced. The greedy and foolish Wall Street and business managers are saved and the good managers end up with taxpayer-financed competitors who should be gone! Goldman Sachs had two of their top people (Rubin and Paulson) in DC as Treasurer for Clinton and Bush, and guess what, their firm got lots of bailout money plus about $30 bill. of the bailout money given to AIG. Talk about favors to friends! Sounds like fraud and theft to me. Our OccupyPeace.us leader, Gerald Celente, was a victim in the MFGlobal failure, where he and other investors had their personal accounts looted to fund a high-risk scheme by the scoundrel CEO, former U.S. Senator Jon Corzine. When he was called to testify in DC, his buddies in Congress accepted his lame excuse that he didn't know where the money went, so he got off with no legal charges! The people are largely ignored in this favor-trading process, and end up paying the bills by taxes and less-valuable money (less purchasing power), while the value of their savings shrink and jobs disappear.

An example of excess, unconstitutional, and unlawful government intervention is Obama's trashing of the rule of law by his unjust allocation of Chrysler assets, where he gave more equity to his friends at the UAW Pension Fund than the legally 'first-in-line' bondholders. This cast a pall on investments in other firms in the future due to buyer's and lender's fear of possible arbitrary theft or dilution by the government.

I recommend that the government stay out of the recovery process and let the free market penalize and eliminate the bad managers with loss of their jobs and trimming or bankruptcy of their firms. Iceland set the example by letting the banks fail, and prosecuting the corrupt managers! (only Iceland did!) This is painful in the short term, but allows recovery to start sooner and better.

'Free Market' is briefly defined as: Little or no government control of pricing, creation of new firms, pay and benefits, hiring and firing, etc., all within the Core Principle in Chapter 3, # 2, and the Constitution. This is the approach preferred by the **'Austrian School' of economic thought** (Hayek, von Mises, Rothbard;in the Glossary), which emphasizes the spontaneous organizing power of free market pricing, decisions by individuals, gold-as-money, and little or no government management or stimulation of the economy. Liberals prefer the **'Keynesian Theory'** (Krugman, Samuelson, Stiglitz; in the Glossary) which depends on massive use of government fiscal (spending) and monetary (interest rates, money supply) policy, both using fake money, to try to create prosperity or avoid and end depressions by 'stimulus' spending. History and logic show the Keynes approach is unsustainable and never works for more than a year or two. Monetary stimulus is like heroin; it gives you a brief high, but has no long-term benefit and can make you sick!

For another definition, I define '**Greed**' (see Glossary) as an excess desire for advantage or benefits that ends up hurting the seeker. Examples are: 1. investing in high-risk securities and losing, or 2. working so hard that you hurt your health and family. This is not to be confused with **'Success'**, where the seeker gains in a productive, lawful, sustainable, and ethical way. Liberals and Progressives often view them as the same. See full definitions in the Glossary.

Obama's national health care system ('The Patient Protection and Affordable Care Act' -PPACA-, or 'ObamaCare') was announced in early 2010, and will take effect through 2014. It will add a huge debt and tax burden, while reducing the quality of health care (rationing of services, delays, impersonal). I know because I have lived in Canada under their system. Read more in Chapter 3, item 8. As shown in Chapter 4, we must revise and repeal many laws to **Restore Peace and Prosperity.**

As described more below, our unique position as **issuer of the primary world reserve currency** (anyone will accept and keep it; good as gold) has allowed us to create trillions of US Dollars (USD) out of thin air to finance subprime mortgages and pay for imports (leading to 'off-shoring' jobs), wars, pork, bailouts, stimulus, etc. This corruption and foolishness could not be done without this flood of fake money. It is the evil root that funds most corruption and abuse. But politicians and bankers love it, so it keeps flowing! This excessive expansion of the money supply ('monetary inflation', like a balloon) reduces the value of all other USD, and risks eventual collapse of its value (when people, firms and nations finally refuse to accept or keep it). The purchasing power (PP) of the USD has dropped by 98% since the Federal Reserve System was created in 1913. The drop has been sharper since Nixon took us off the last remnants of the gold standard (which limits excess creation of USD) in 1971. Government and private spending has zoomed up since 1971 as new money flooded our economy. Prices go up as the Dollar's value (PP) goes down, and wages seldom keep up with the higher prices. On a personal level, this is why we see more wives working to help meet family expenses.

The U.S. National debt (Treasury Bills and Bonds) is now over $18 trillion. It grew by leaps with the 'Quantitative Easing' (QE) bailouts and stimulus programs which ran from 2008 to 2014! Worse, this does not count the 'off-budget', unfunded, over $14 trillion dollar future liabilities of Social Security and $97 trillion for Medicare (see Table 1). These debts can only be paid by; 1) massive creation of more dollars (which will reduce the value of all dollars, and cause an inflationary depression!!), or 2) Default by repudiation! We are 'stuck between a rock and a hard place', and only a major reduction in spending and benefits will solve the problem (if ever).

The nations that accumulate USDs from payments for exports to us, once used them to buy our government debt ('Treasuries'; T-Bills, bonds, etc.) as a way to earn some interest, but we now often pay zero interest!

Of foreign holders of US debt, China is the largest holder, with $1.712 trillion in June-2015, and Japan is next at $1.197 trillion. Total foreign holdings are $6.013 trillion. Both Japan and China want to keep the value of the dollar high when compared to their own currencies. That helps their exports to the United States seem more affordable, which helps their economies grow. To that end, China devalued its currency by almost 2 % in Aug-2015. That's why, despite China's occasional threats to sell its holdings, both countries are happy to be America's biggest foreign bankers. As of Aug-2015, China had about $2.3 trillion invested in USD denominated assets (the world's biggest holder), of which about half are in Treasuries. This is about 70% of China's total reserves (down from 80% in 2002), and they are starting to use them to buy hard assets (mines, oil/gas rights, land, buildings) worldwide to avoid losses as value of the USD drops. Maybe they will buy the U.S. Congress next? Like all politicians, most are 'for sale', as discussed below.

The abuse by the USA of its monetary system by monetary inflation (creating new money to pay bills) is a major world concern, and was the main topic of the April-2009, and Nov-2010 meetings of the G20. Other nations are looking for ways to avoid dependency on, and ownership of, USDs. A flight to safety is starting, and could lead to a collapse in USD value (fake money requires demand to keep its PP). Russia and China have suggested the USD be replaced as the reserve currency by a 'basket' of several currencies, or Special Drawing Rights, managed by the International Monetary Fund (IMF). At the Oct-2015 'every 5 years' IMF meeting in Lima, Peru, **China made good progress in trying to include their Yuan in the 'basket'! (see details on p. 116)**. The BRICS (Brazil, Russia, India, China, and South Africa) started trading with each other in their own currencies in 2011, thus reducing demand for the USD, and speeding its fall in value! If we keep creating new money (inflate the money supply), 1. The USD will crash in purchasing power (PP), 2. We will not be able to afford foreign purchases with our soon near-worthless paper money, and 3. We will pay existing foreign debts with the same near-worthless paper money. This is debt default by hyperinflation. No country wants this to happen, especially our creditors and holders of cash and USD denominated assets. Thus they discuss alternatives for a smooth departure from the current dependency on the USD as the primary reserve currency for world trade.

As discussed in Chapter 2, Empire-USA is an expensive and damaging part of our foreign policy. On May 8, 2009, Ivan Eland Ph.D. (Independent.org) wrote in his article, **'How the US Empire Contributed to the Economic Crisis'**, "*A few — and only a few — prescient commentators have questioned whether the U.S. can sustain its informal global empire in the wake of the most severe economic crisis since World War II. And the simultaneous quagmires in Iraq and Afghanistan are leading more and more opinion leaders and taxpayers to* *this question. But the U.S. Empire helped cause the meltdown in the first place.*

These observations also tie in with the section below; 'Fake Money: How it Funds Wars and Corruption'.

In the political arena, we find most Congresspersons, party leaders, and 'loyalist' workers (at all levels; DC, State and County) of the major political parties have failed the people, and should reform or be replaced! The priority of most of them is to keep their Party jobs and social and business connections! They want to be viewed as 'normal' and 'loyal', so they are obedient, follow-the-leader, party-first, and denounce critics of their Party and its leaders as wierdos, conspiracy theorists, and disloyal troublemakers. I observe that over 90% of US citizens who vote pick the person they think will help get them what they want from government (cash, benefits, legal favors, etc.). The same applies to campaign donors who expect a payback if their candidate is elected (they often donate to both opposing candidates). The Main-Stream-Media (MSM) follows the same cowardly path (to avoid offense to subscribers and advertisers).

Those nation-first, people-first, 'comply with the Constitution' rebels who dare to question the Party Lines are shunned and ridiculed. Thus the misconduct of those in power gets worse, and the Party declines in membership and at the polls. The Party leaders toe-the-line to avoid disturbing the party's 'image', and upsetting major campaign donors, most of whom profit or grow from war, subsidies, and special laws and rulings. As an activist for better (less) government since 1978, I have watched with dismay as the Republican party was taken-over since 1988 by far-right warmonger 'neoconservatives' and the religious-right. This created the 'Big Government Conservative' concept with its spending and pre-emptive Mideast wars (Afghan, Iraq, Libya; Iran soon?) for oil, empire, and defense of Israel, all of which violate the Constitution. The Heritage Foundation, where Steve Forbes is a Trustee, is an example. They awarded the liar, murderer Dick Cheney their highest honor for his promotion of conservative values. Now with Obama in power, the left-wing antiwar crowd is silent as he invades and kills, because they are getting the welfare benefits they want.

These wars are an abuse of our troops, because they are for political and economic goals, not defense (same for Vietnam). They were started based on lies (see Appendix 1 and 2). The 'official' 9/11 report is full of voids and bias. For example, the report states that 13 of the 17 9/11 bombers were Saudis, so why didn't we invade Saudi Arabia?? Well, it's because we already had a deal for their oil, and we wanted a reason to invade other countries to get their oil and build pipelines! A hidden reason was to prevent oil sales to China, and thus limit their growth and power.

Our role as the world's policeman (or 'Boss'), and ruler of 'Empire USA' are huge issues that need to be discussed. Just as with Rome, and all other empires in history (see Chapter 2), the expense of wars abroad and welfare at home caused their failure. The USA is on the brink, and I show my plan to **'Restore Peace and Prosperity'** in Chapter 4.

Corruption of government speed-up when voters find they can elect people who will give them benefits paid by someone else. I oppose the government handing-out favors to anyone, liberal or conservative, business or personal. They are all un-constitutional and depend on funding from gang-theft-by-vote, or fake money (a hidden tax), and usually do more harm than good (if you count side effects). I follow the Core Principle shown in Chapter 3, Item 2 (and below in this chapter) which says the government should only 'protect rights', which means 'natural rights' and the Constitution, not 'legislated rights' (such as free health care, school, subsidies, etc.) that should be repealed.

Most elected officials, especially in Congress with its unlimited supply of fake money, will do almost anything to keep their plush and powerful jobs. The pork, earmark grants, subprime loans, and favors to campaign donors are part of their career planning. Rome called it 'bread and circuses'. Their failure to end the tragic and illegal Iraq and Afghan wars during the 2006 to 2008 Democratic 'mandate' years is a shameful example. It seems the Democrats would rather have thousands more people die (our troops and many times more local civilians) than be blamed for a messy withdrawal, or be accused of 'surrender' after our illegal, immoral invasion and occupation. Shame on them!!

Excess spending and debt loomed as threats to the U.S. economy, and Congress and Bush ignored the problems! These chickens came home to roost in 2008 with election of Obama. More and more State projects are funded (pork, grants) and controlled by the federal government because it never runs out of fake money. The state politicians beg for it and states' rights get weaker due to the strings attached. For more info on money, go to Chapter 4.

Neocon warmongers drove our foreign policy in the G.W. Bush years. The 'Project for a New American Century' (PNAC, www.newamericancentury.org) was founded by 'use more power' pushers such as neocons Cheney, Rumsfeld, Perle, Kristol, Abrams, Feith, and the like, and their plan, a white paper produced in September of 1997 entitled "Rebuilding America's Defenses: Strategy, Forces and Resources for a New Century" depended on war to defend and expand Empire-USA control world-wide. It became the blueprint for the Bush team to invade Iraq and Afghanistan (for oil, Israel, and bases). The 9/11 tragedy was the trigger they needed! (see items 4 and 6 in Chapter 3). In Mar-2009 they changed their name to 'The Foreign

Policy Initiative' (www.foreignpolicyi.org) with the same plans to grow Empire-USA. Watch them get funding from the military-industrial folks! Many neocons are Israel-First Zionists (and all are Empire builders), which means they put the success of Israel before the USA, and expect the USA to pay for its defense with our blood and treasure. The Israeli lobby AIPAC (American-Israel Public Affairs Committee, www.aipac.org) should be registered as a foreign lobby (they claim it is a USA org!), and thus disclose its finances, as those of UK and France are; another special exception for Israel. If a Congressperson doesn't support Israel, they don't get re-elected!! AIPAC attacks them, or supports their opponent. Take note that most Congresspersons (plus the President, VP, Secretary of State, etc.) attend their annual banquet in DC and kiss-up by promising vast military and financial support for Israel!!. Only a retiring Congressperson will criticize AIPAC. Its intervention in USA affairs is a massive scandal!! No cries of anti-Semitism please; this is a legal, political and financial issue, not religious. For more go to: http://original.antiwar.com/giraldi/2009/05/18/picking-on-aipac/

G. W. Bush and his team 'used' 9/11 and their 'War on Terror' to justify a long list of excess powers for the Executive branch, plus a host of violations of domestic laws and liberties (domestic spying, excess control of travel – TSA, torture and jailing of 'non-combatants', etc.). More at issues 4 and 5 in Chapter 3.

My Plan to Restore Peace and Prosperity

This is a summary of the detailed plan in Chapter 4. Government spending has soared since Nixon abrogated the Bretton Woods Monetary Treaty, and imposed price controls, in 1971, and needs new leadership and reform at all levels. They now condone or promote 'more-government' for war, spending, religion, illegal immigration, unconstitutional restriction of rights, illegal 'signing statements' that change laws, illegal Executive Orders that start wars, torture, and corruption! Some say suspensions of rights are 'needed for a while'; Nonsense, the free market and rule of law work best, and the rights rarely come back once ignored!

The religious-right and neoconservative warmongers now dominate the Republican Party, and push for imposing their views on all of us by use of the coercive powers of government. I oppose 'using' the government as a tool to impose one's personal preferences (not legal principles) on others, and will work to restore key principles such as shown below to 'defend rights', not 'control personal choices'. I recommend:

1) Limited Constitution-based government emphasizing sound money, personal responsibility, Liberty, property rights, low taxing and spending, and a non-interventionist foreign policy, with a strong defense against homeland attack and valid threats,
2) No wars (or 'Police actions') without the express approval of Congress,
3) No pre-emptive wars or invasions,
4) Use war only for defense of homeland from invasions or proven threats. No foreign wars or invasions for economic or political goals (such as for oil, land, defense of Israel, and Empire-USA; see Appendix 1), and
5) Repeal unconstitutional and unnecessary restrictions on liberty and privacy, and Executive Branch power-grabs, such as the Patriot Act, and the Military Commissions Act, and restore Habeas Corpus.

We should support the idea: **'When our leaders 'go bad' and hijack our government, we must fight to reform or replace them!** '

It is time to repudiate the misconduct, and violation of the Constitution, by our 'leaders', and start an honest rebuilding plan for more peace, liberty, and prosperity. Rather than continuing the present leadership's mode of avoidance and denial, this honest approach will achieve needed changes.

Fighting the system is hard, but I predict Ghandhi's aphorism will prevail: **"First they ignore you, then they ridicule you, then they fight you, then you win."**

Core Principle - All of my 'Issue Positions' are based on the following objective principle**: 'The government's proper role is to protect the personal and property rights of its citizens, as individuals, from threat or violation by others'**. This is consistent with the federal constitution. History and logic show that this approach yields not only more liberty, but more peace, prosperity, ethics, and justice. See more in Chapter 3, Item 2.

Fake Money Funds Wars and Corruption

Wars are expensive and the USA has a special advantage as issuer of the world's primary reserve currency so it can create money out of thin-air. Thus we have had more wars **(less peace)** since our money achieved this status soon after World War1. I recommend sound money; coins made of, or paper notes redeemable for, precious metals such as gold and silver (as required by Article 1, Section 10, of our constitution).

I now present a summary of our monetary system, and its problems. See more in my published articles in Appendix 2. Note that I use the terms 'money' and 'currency' as synonymous.

After years of successful free-market money (most of 1792 to 1913), the unconstitutional Federal Reserve System (a privately-owned bank; they used 'System' since some politicians oppose central banks) was created in 1913 'by

and for' politicians and bankers, so they never run out of money! This gave the federal government a monopoly (via legal tender laws) on creation and 'management' of both metallic and paper money, with the announced purpose of protecting its value. The Feds' so-called 'mandates';1) stable currency value, and 2) high employment, are fake ways to attract citizen support (and they have failed at both!). Note that since 1913, the US Dollar (USD) has lost 98% of its value (purchasing power) due to excessive creation of new, additional, money (monetary inflation)!!
In 1933 FDR was worried that, 1) People would avoid use of his low-value paper money, and 2) Foreign countries were concerned about our lack of gold reserves and might start redeeming paper dollars for gold, so by an illegal Executive Order #1602 in 1933 he forced all citizens to submit their gold coins and bullion to the government for $20.67 per ounce in paper dollars. Then he decreased the amount of gold backing each paper dollar by illegally re-setting the price of gold to $35 oz. A ripoff! They used part of this profit to fund the Exchange Stabilization Fund (ESF) with $2 bill. which was part of the Gold Reserve Act of 1934. The ESF allows the US Treasurer, by his signature only, to 'play the gold market' to keep the price down, so the USD looks better! In 1944 the winners of WW2 met at a resort hotel in the Bretton Woods area of Vermont and agreed that only nations could exchange paper money for gold (the 'Bretton Woods' agreement), and the USD was declared the primary reserve currency. In 1965 LBJ ended use of silver in coins and used cheaper copper and nickel alloys. The pre-1965 coins ('junk silver') now sell for their bullion value. Then Nixon abrogated the Bretton Woods Agreement in August, 1971 due to our serious financial problems such as; a) We were running out of gold because France and other countries were converting their 'EuroDollars' to gold (USD accumulated in Europe due to our imports from there); b) The US was poor after spending on Vietnam and LBJ's 'Great Society', etc. Under this pressure, Nixon illegally 'floated' the USD (no fixed-price for

gold; no fixed exchange rates with foreign currency), and ended convertibility to gold by any person or government. This meant the US could make dollars out of thin air at will, and did we ever! Whoopee! With USD no longer 'good as gold', the currency of all other nations lost their gold 'backing' and also became fiat by default.

The Fed increased the basic money supply (cash in circulation; M0) from $622 bill. in 2000 to $3,978 bill. in 2015 (a 640% increase, while GDP increased only 86%!) to recover from the dot.com bubble. This became the underlying cause of the 2007 housing bubble burst as it funded the CRA, Fannie, Freddie, Ginnie Mae, and Main Street and Wall Street binges of excessive spending and high-risk credit. Economists call this funding a 'moral hazard'. The QE-1 'Bernanke Spike' of $2 trill. in late 2008 was to stimulate the economy after the housing bubble burst in 2007. Then QE-2, and in Sep-2012 QE-3 spending $40 bn per mo. on mortgage-based securities, plus the existing 'Operation Twist' of $45 bn mo., which finally ended in Oct-2014! Constant meddling !

The Fed destroys the value of our money by excess expansion of money supply ('monetary inflation'). Simple examples are that a family car cost about $2,000 in the 1970's and is $20,000 today. A night in 'Motel 6' was $6 in the '70's and is $45 to $60 now.

There were large 'dollar' supply increases from 2000 to 2009, which contributed to the bubble that burst in 2007. A decline in purchasing power of the dollar followed this increase in the money supply.
The main purpose of convertibility of paper (or electronic dollars) to gold is to prevent excess expansion of the money supply (monetary 'inflation') by the government, and thus reduction in purchasing power. Without convertibility, this 'easy money' is an unlimited 'piggy-bank' and credit card for the government. While the USA was a heavy

spender since after WW1 in 1919, this unlimited supply of 'no gold' money has allowed faster increases in government spending and debt for wars, welfare, and pork since 1971.

Table 1 shows the results of this money creation, spending and debt. Note that much of it is hidden or unfunded to help politicians keep their jobs!

Table 1
The Honest National Debt and Unfunded Liabilities

A. $ 18.406 tn National Debt (disclosed debt)

B.	56.740	Misc. unfunded Liabilities ('off- budget')
	27.563	Medicare A, B, and D (unfunded)
	14.366	Social Security (unfunded)

$ 98.669 trillion   Total for B

$ 117.075 trillion = Grand Total (A+B)

(Source: USDebtClock.org, Oct. 14, 2015)

Notes: 1) Liabilities are unfunded promises based on current tax and funding inputs and on projections using these assumptions and future demographic shifts in U.S. population, 2) National (public) debt is; a. the face or principal amount of all securities (marketable and unmarketable – owned by Fed -) currently outstanding, b. military and civilian pensions, c. retiree health benefits, and d. other guarantees and obligations. (source; www.USDebtClock.org).

The 'official' government debt figures ignore the above Medicare, Soc. Sec. and Misc. items (treated as 'off-budget' !!), plus potential trillions that loom due to losses at Fannie and Freddie, now government-owned.

In 1970 the national debt was $380.9 bill. (about $3.4 tn in 2015 dollars), and 37.6% of GDP. As of Oct. 12, 2015, national debt was $18.4 Trill. and 103% of GDP! (www.usgovernmentspending.com, and USDebtClock.org) All economists agree that debt over 100% of GDP is dangerous! No one believes the debt will be paid. Overt default (refusal to pay; repudiation) of most of it is one strategy. Another is creating new fake money, but this would likely cause hyper price inflation, and destroy the US Dollar and economy. Horrible choices, and all thanks to irresponsible government leaders.

Of course consumer (personal) debt (cars, home mortgages, credit cards, TVs, student loans, etc.) zoomed upward because of the easy (lax terms, subprime), cheap (low interest) fake money created by the Fed in 2000 to 2014, and is now about $17 tn ; just under the National debt)! As more people lose their jobs, more bills go unpaid, and the defaults and foreclosures are now doing the upward zoom. Sad.

The government is broke, yet the 'political' spending persists! Governors and Congresspersons seek Federal money for all manner of State projects, but it comes with strings attached, which lets the DC folks control many aspects of State functions (Bye-Bye to States Rights; see Appendix 2).

Prices started their 'hockey stick' shaped rise a few years after Nixon severed the Dollar's ties to gold in 1971 as the effect of excess money and spending trickled to the world economy. Within in a few years, all nations worldwide ceased convertibility, even the prudent Swiss floated the Swiss Franc (CHF), but have been less abusive than others; hence while 1 USD=about 4 CHF in 1961, it is now about 1 US=1 CHF, so they only inflated by 2.5 while by 2008 the US inflated by 10; 4 times more! The USA has been the worst abuser among developed nations (older countries remembered their lessons from past monetary failures). The US has created so much new 'free, fake money' since 1971 that the USD has lost about 80% of its purchasing power (this excess expansion of the money supply causes 'price inflation', like a balloon, because each dollar is worth less) with its consequent price increases. Check prices of common 'commodity' items that are not imported, subsidized, cheaper due to new technology, or under price control, such as a pizza, or a restaurant meal. A good example is that a room at 'Motel 6' cost $6 in the '50s and is now in the $60 range in 2015 (same type of room and service). There is your 10X loss of USD value! This goes along with a 95% loss since the Federal Reserve monopoly was created in 1913! **The only reason we can get away with this is because the USD is the world's 'reserve currency' (any person or bank will accept it as payment, and keep it as if 'good as gold'), but the era of USA world dominance is ending (see Chapter 4).**

What is the solution? My 'Restore Peace and Prosperity' plan in Chapter 4 says; Cut spending, Abolish the Federal Reserve System, and Legal Tender laws, and go to 'free market banking' (no government monopoly on money), and the 'Private Gold Standard' (p. 153). Why Gold? To achieve broad use as a medium of exchange, commodity coins must be made of, or contain, a material that has these ten characteristics:

1) Rare, with a low amount in existence now, and limited new supply.
2) Malleable; can be pressed/stamped into coins,
3) Durable; Stable physically and chemically; doesn't break, rust, or rot; can be stored; lasts through much handling,
4) Easy to identify, and determine purity and weight,
5) Difficult or impossible to counterfeit,
6) Homogeneous; a piece is the same throughout,
7) Divisible into pieces; diamonds and pearls aren't,
8) High value per ounce; not bulky to handle or store,
9) Acceptable to most Sellers; familiar and saleable,
10) Has market value when not used as money. Thus;

a. is equal in value to the items in a transaction, and

b. is a store and measure of value.

The 'market' (users of money) has decided that gold fits these requirements best, but silver and copper can have a role in parallel, with no fixed ratios set as to value per gram (i.e., no bi-metallic standard). The coins must be valued and marked by weight of their precious metal content (such as 'milligrams'), or base-metal 'tokens' (made of zinc, steel, etc.) for the amount they can be redeemed for. Paper notes are OK for convenience, but they are only a claim check for redemption in gold by the issuing mint.

Note that a nation, or market area, **never 'runs out of gold' –except due to excessive imports- because gold APPRECIATES in purchasing power with an increase in local demand (a growing economy), and a limited supply of gold.**

The conversion of the US monetary system to gold will be a massive project, but if we don't start soon, the USD will crash in value (by 50% or more) as people, merchants, and governments worldwide refuse to accept or keep it. More in Appendix 2. To those who join the team at **OccupyPeace.us** in the fight for more peace, liberty and personal responsibility, I say: '**Thanks, we must never give up.'**

Best regards, Dave Redick

Chapter 2

Empire-USA: The Wars and Failures

The analysis shown below explains why all empires, and 'Imperial Style' governments, in history have failed, and why our 'Empire-USA' faces the same fate. The only question is whether the people and government of the USA have the wisdom and will to engage in a 'Managed Decline' by terminating the empire and imperial conduct on their own schedule, rather than by chaotic crash of the US Dollar, economy, and lifestyle. Take notice of the 'Solutions' section in Part C below.

The Phases of an Empire

Part A: Key Points

* **An Empire is a nation that; 1. Owns and occupies colonies, and/or 2. Controls, or has great influence over, other nations**. Empires require economic and military strength to start and maintain, and this is expensive.

* **All Empires fail, and for the same reasons:** 1. Expense of military abroad, and subsidies at home, 2. Decline in domestic productivity (spoiled, parasitic citizens), and 3. Corruption (illegal conduct) and decadence and abuse (immoral conduct; fraud, theft, etc.) by leaders and citizens.

* **Empire-USA, Our Deal to other nations is:** 'We will be the world's policeman and protect you, but you must accept our fake money and 'influence'. With our spending for over 800 bases in 130 countries, the USA is far into Phase 3-Failure. Look around you for the symptoms shown in Part B-3 and Part C below.

Part B: Events/Symptoms in each Phase

Phase 1- Growth (shown on Figure 1 on page 33)

* Land: Gain territory by 'discovery' (too bad for the natives), or conquest.

* Strength: Start growth of economic and military strength. Sound money (precious metal, or redeemable paper).

* Government: New land is governed as a colony or part of homeland nation (becoming a sovereign republic may require a revolution).

* Ethics: Most government people and citizens are hard-working and honest. Government is a 'servant'.

Phase 2- Maturation

* Land: Add contiguous land, or remote colonies, by conquest, annexation (Hawaii), or negotiation.

* Strength: Become a world leader in both economic and military strength. Homeland receives cheap imports from colonies. Currency is debased to allow more government spending, without raising taxes.

* Government: Grows stronger and acts as boss, manager, nanny, owner, etc. Power is used to 'manage' other nations to impose/protect the Empire's 'interests'.

* Ethics: Corruption and decadence start to grow due to decline in personal responsibility caused by nanny state.

Figure 1: The Phases of an Empire

Curve Height Shows Combined Military and Economic Strength (Power and Wealth), with dates for the USA.

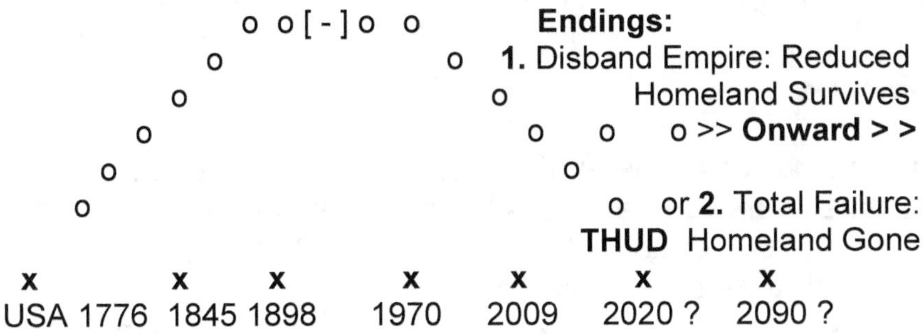

```
      o o[-]o  o          Endings:
         o              o   1. Disband Empire: Reduced
       o                o        Homeland Survives
     o                o   o    o >> Onward > >
   o                      o
 o                              o   or 2. Total Failure:
                            THUD  Homeland Gone
 x       x    x       x      x      x       x
USA 1776 1845 1898    1970   2009   2020 ?  2090 ?
```

Phase 1, Growth - Phase 2, Mature - Phase 3, Decline or Fail

Phase 3- Decline and/or Failure

* Land: Lose colonies (or control of other nations) by revolution or voluntary release (due to expense and unrest). Uses more aggressive military control to suppress complaints

* Strength: No longer a world leader. Power declines by 50% or more. Value of fake currency crashes in purchasing power by 50% or more. Default on debt (or pay-off with low value paper currency).

* Government: Gets weak and desperate. Leaders try to gain power to survive citizen discontent. Laws and police become more aggressive in suppressing complaints. 'Bread and Circuses' grow, now called grants, subsidies, stimulus, and entitlements.

* Ethics: Corruption and decadence are rampant in both social and government conduct. Empire failure occurs as

33

either; A. Nation survives, but at a reduced level of strength and standard of living (England, France, Italy, Spain, and Russia are examples; see list in Part D), or B. Ceases to exist due to takeover by other nations or groups.

Part C: Empire-USA is in Phase 3: Decline or Failure

Problems:

* High Expenses: The expense to maintain bases, and fight wars, worldwide exceeds the monetary and political benefits. As of Oct-2015, the US has over 800 military bases, with troops (not counting embassies), in 130 countries, and acts as the world's policeman (Boss?) to protect its 'interests', and impose 'influence'. Resistance by our 'subjects' is building. Military expenses are a drag on the economy, and the troops get less than ideal equipment due to cost problems. Host nations are unhappy having our occupying troops.

* High Debt: The US is a bankrupt Empire by any measure. It cannot hope to pay back the about $6 trillion in debt held by other nations, or the about $99 trillion unfunded future obligations of domestic programs (Medicare, Social Security, etc.; See Table 1, p.27). Interest payments are large now, and will become unpayable when (not if) the Fed is obliged to increase interest rates (to attract buyers)!. As of late 2015 the US Dollar (USD) is still the world's primary 'reserve currency' (used and held as 'good as gold' by other nations; it can be viewed as a share in 'USA Inc.'), but declining in its percent use worldwide (was 90%, now about 70%) because the US is also the world's biggest debtor, and has high deficits. **This combination of 'fiat' paper currency (not made of, or convertible to, gold or silver) with reserve status has never occurred before in history!** Thus, since all US government debt is denominated in USD, the government can create new low-value dollars out of thin air to pay its debts! A new form of default! The USD is in a precarious position due to excessive expansion of the money supply ('monetary inflation') and the USD could crash in value at any time. The extreme is 'price hyperinflation', when the money becomes almost worthless. As with heroin, lots of fake money (the Federal Reserve Bank calls it 'liquidity' or 'quantitative easing') feels good at first, but has withdrawal pain called recession or depression. Since the federal government never runs out of money, it often becomes the funder for state projects (with strings attached, called 'control'), and 'states rights' wither. This gives vote-getting power to Congressmen, and acquiescent State officials suck it up to avoid taxing to raise state funds.

* **Enemies:** The US claims to be a 'world leader', but this is often a cover to be a bully to control other countries with an occupying force to gain land and resources (mostly oil). Trust and respect for the US has declined in the eyes of its citizens and other nations. Other nations are now less dependent on a weaker US not always willing to follow our orders. AT home, citizen unrest causes the federal government to grasp for new, unconstitutional power.

* **Corruption and Bad Ethics:** Ethics and social conduct are on the decline in the US. Corruption is rampant in both the government and business. Shady conduct is considered 'normal' (gang theft by vote, 'earmark' pork handouts, lying, etc.). Prime time TV is now riddled with sexual content, cursing, glorification of misconduct, and violence. Sports are riddled with violence (the fans like it!) and cheating (or umpires ignore rules), condoned by coaches and team owners that want to sell more tickets. Little or none of the above occurred in the '50s. It is typical conduct in a failing empire, as social mores decline.

Solutions:

Of the two ways to end the inevitable Phase 3 of an Empire (Decline or Failure), it is far less painful to engage in a 'managed decline', or 'nation restoration', compared to a massive depression. England and France are examples. A 'managed' process is shown in my "**Restore Peace and Prosperity'** plan in Chapter 4, which includes prompt action to;

1. Invoke a major **change in foreign policy** by; a. Terminating Empire-USA, and its role as policeman and bully of the world, and focus on homeland defense; b Reducing spending and conflict by closing most, or all, overseas bases, and keeping only a minimal standing army (primarily State-controlled National Guard); c. Stop creating enemies by meddling in the affairs of other nations by force, sanctions, or bribery (no preemptive wars or occupations); and d. Promote free trade.

2. Invoke a similar **change in domestic policy** where; a. Federal spending is reduced by 50% or more; b. Creation of new fake money is ended; c. Sound money is introduced (paper is convertible to precious metal), and the Federal Reserve System is abolished; d. The Constitution and law are adhered to (with repeal of recent bad laws); and e. Market intervention (favors to firms, unions, people) is ended, and free enterprise capitalism is used.

These steps would help bring the government back to its proper role to; **'Protect the personal and property rights of citizens, as individuals, from threat or violation by others'**. With this approach, the USA and its citizens would enjoy a future of peace, prosperity, justice and good ethics. It always works! I cite W. Germany in 1948, and later Ireland, Prov. of Alberta, Canada, and New Zealand.

Part D: The History of Empire Phases

Sources: 1. 'An Inquiry into the Decline and Fall of Nations', W. Playfair, England, 1805 (Rare books library, Toronto, Canada), 2. 'Empire of Debt', Bonner and Wiggins, 2006

Name	Start Phase 1	End Phase 3	Total Years	Status
Babylonian	1792 bc	1752 bc	300	gone
Assyrian	900 bc	612 bc	288	gone
Carthage	800 bc	100 bc	700	gone
Persian	648 bc	330 bc	318	gone, Iran surv'd
Athenian-Greek	500 bc	300 bc	200	gone
Macedonian	338 bc	309 bc	29	gone
Chinese	221 bc	1912	233	Homeland survived
Roman	573 bc	476	1,049	gone, split to. Byzantine & Holy Roman
Byzantine	1054	1453	399	gone
Arabian	630	1258	628	gone
Holy Roman	800	1806	1006	gone
Portuguese	1495	1975	480	Homeland survived
Mongol	1206	1920	714	gone, Mongolia surv'd
Abyssinian	1270	1974	704	gone
Ottoman	1281	1923	642	gone, Turkey survived
Spanish	1492	1975	483	Homeland survived
British	1500	1950	450	Homeland survived
French	1600	1965	365	Homeland survived
Dutch	1627	1944	317	Homeland survived
Austro-Hung.	1804	1918	114	Austria and Hung. surv'd
USA	1845	(active)	167 +	In Ph. 3; #1 world power
German	1884	1918	34	Homeland survived
Japanese	1871	1945	76	Homeland survived

Chapter 3: Key Issues

All of the issues discussed below are part of my "**Restore Peace and Prosperity'** plan, as discussed further in Chapter 4. I comment on 33 topics below, but there could be many more. Send suggestions and comments to me at RedickD@aol.com. Thanks

Most of the statements below are lengthy in order to be complete. However, if you just read the first 10 or 15 lines, you will have read the main points.

Contents of Chapter 3:

For information on other issues, please contact me at RedickD@aol.com. I appreciate your interest.

****

1. The Constitution:

We have observed many examples of people (including some in government who should know better) treating the Constitution as a set of laws and rules that control citizens. Wrong! The purpose of the Constitution is to decree what the government must, may, and may not do, by making it a short list of 'enumerated powers'. Congress (the Legislature) makes the laws! That's one of the reasons the 18th amendment (alcohol prohibition) was wrong, it put restrictions on the people. The same applies to a proposed amendment for abortion. Such issues should be passed as laws at the state level, or not at all (if unconstitutional, or **none of the government's business, as is true of most things**). It is the job of us citizens, and our elected 'leaders', to maintain those limits and keep the government (at ALL levels) on a short leash. The intent was, 'if it is not on the list, the government can't do it!' Many Founders, led by George Mason, balked even at this restraint. They didn't trust the government (and its power-seeking elected members) to stay within the limits, so they wouldn't support ratification until a 'Bill of Rights' (the first ten amendments) to protect the rights of the people and States was included. They were right! The Constitution has been abused to gain power for Federal politicians and their friends. Today, more than half of laws and spending are unconstitutional. Abuse of the 'implied powers', 'general welfare', and 'interstate commerce' provisions account for most deviations. A further misunderstanding is that we are a Democracy. Wrong. In a Democracy the citizens vote directly to make laws, and tyranny of the majority soon rules. We are a Constitutional Republic, where we vote for Representatives who in turn are restricted by the Constitution.

A 'short leash' is required on government power at all levels (city, county, state, federal) because we grant them 'police powers' (legal use of force by police and military) which is easily abused. The current 'War on Terror' and 'Patriot Act' are good examples of abuse.

2. Dave's Core Principle:
Most elected officials take positions based on their feelings, personal preferences, and pressure from the special interest groups who give them money or votes. All of my positions are based on an **objective principle,** which is:

"The proper role of government is to PROTECT the personal and property rights of its citizens, as INDIVIDUALS, from violation or threat by OTHERS."

With this approach, government ownership and control is minimized, and human interaction is more peaceful and voluntary (it pays to get along!), and has a proven track record of producing more liberty, peace, prosperity, morality, and justice, **proportional to the extent it is employed.**

If so, why do people support 'more-government' systems known as **Progressive, Liberal, or Socialist?** The key is they hope to fund their projects with 'other people's money' by 'tax the rich' schemes. **While popular (most people like to have others pay for their benefits), these systems use inherently immoral and coercive 'gang theft by vote' taxation, which results in declining peace, productivity, and justice, if you count all the side-effects** (including robbing 'the rich' by forced payment of their so-called 'fair share'). Liberals-Progressives purposely ignore that the top 10 percent of income earners pay about 70 percent of all federal income taxes though they earn only 43 percent of all income. Isn't that enough?? The bottom 50 percent pay only 2 percent of income taxes but earn 13 percent of total income. About half of tax filers paid no federal income tax at all. Note it is 'dollars' that count, not 'percentages'! A society that broadly accepts this type of immoral funding is in decline, as shown by falling morality in all parts of US activity since the 1950s. Sad!

Key points to understanding and using my Core Principle are:
a) Our Federal and State governments were created by, and are still controlled by, 'we the people'
to protect our rights (a short list of 'natural rights' you are born with, which does not include subsidized or free health care, education, etc.). Thus, **the government is our servant, not our owner, manager, funder, or nanny.**
To implement this protection (enforce the laws), we grant the government 'police powers' (the right to use force), and thus we need to be ever on guard to avoid abuse, including use of laws beyond their intended purpose (RICO, FISA, etc.). For individuals, the flip side of this is; "A person should never initiate force except in self-defense", or **" Persons can do whatever they want to, short of violating the equal rights of others"**. In a personal (not legal) context, I suggest that each person has a moral obligation to be a beneficial presence in the world, and not offensive to others. This starts with being honest, kind, courteous and clean.

Personal rights are freedom of religion, speech, etc. Some of these are listed in the Constitution, but in fact all. are 'natural' at birth, and not bestowed by the government (which can only protect or abuse them; not create, except for contrived 'legislated' rights). Our Founders debated if any should be listed (to avoid exclusion of some not listed), hence they included Amendment IX. Note that only a human individual has personal rights.

Notice that 1. Words like 'manage our money, social system, and economy', 'mother', and 'police the world' are not included in the Principle, and 2. We are not 'created equal' as to mind, body and circumstances, but all citizens have equal rights under the law.

Property includes tangibles, and intellectual property owned by a person or legal organization (corporation, etc.). Except for government restrictions (often unconstitutional), a property right is; " The right to use and dispose of your property (use, sell, loan, lease, give, etc.) however you see fit, short of violating the equal rights of others."
Property rights need to be treated as superior to personal rights in order to avoid conflicts. For example, if you enter someone's property without permission (trespassing) and start to give a sermon, your freedom of speech and religion are not being violated if you are made to leave.

b) The government needs police, courts, and military for national DEFENSE to do its job, all used within the limits of the Constitution. But note that the military must not be used to enforce or solve political or economic issues abroad, when there is no threat to our homeland (such as the Vietnam, Iraq, Afghan and Libyan wars).

c) There are no group rights (by sex, race, age, etc.). Every citizen has the same rights. We should not create 'preferred minorities' with special privileges, which are easily abused.

There should be no subjective versions of laws, such as a 'Hate Crimes'. Theft is theft, murder, is murder.

d) Nothing can be a right if you expect someone else to pay for even part of it (such as health, education, etc.). Insurance is a method to share risks and expenses, but must be voluntary, or if run as a 'single payer' by the government, have equal benefits to all, based on terms and payments, and not include a 'welfare' aspect where some members pay less for the same coverage. For example, using property tax to pay for public schools is a rip-off of owners since there is no connection to whether the payer has kids in school (but it is convenient politically!).

e) Your body is your property. If you hurt yourself, or put yourself at risk, it is none of the government's business. Note that the Core principle above ends in 'by others'.

f) The same principle of 'protection' applies to the property rights of business and other legal entities.

g) As with people, the government has no authorization to be the **'owner, manager, funder, or nanny'** of the 'national economy'. Free enterprise does a great job of supplying goods and services, while government interference (controls, subsidies, etc.) always do more harm than good, if all the side-effects (including inflation and depressions) are counted.

h) Provision of 'essential services' conflicts with the principle of only 'protecting rights', and is a constant threat to limiting the size of government at all levels (city, county, state, and federal). This is where the federal 'General Welfare' clause is most abused. While most should be 'privatized', to the extent these projects (such as education, sewer, water, roads, public health, parks, mass transit, etc.) are unfortunately approved, they should at least be;

1. Charged to users at compensatory rates (user fees, tuition, no subsidies). Again, voluntary private charity can help the truly needy.

2. Built and operated by contractors on a competitive-bid basis. . The main reason the Federal government has become huge, and involved in running or financing so many unconstitutional state and city projects, is that unlike the States and cities, **it never runs out of money, thanks to the Federal Reserve** piggy-bank of fake money!

i) The above Core Principle refers to '**violation or threat by OTHERS'.** The government only has a role to act when such violations or threats are imposed on someone, and they have no choice to avoid it. For example, non-smokers can avoid privately-owned places that allow smoking (bars, etc; just don't go there!), so it would be a violation of the owner's property rights to impose a non-smoking ordinance, but not City Hall (there is only one, and there are times when you are required to go there; no choice), or other government sites. However, while it is improper to use the legal system to impose your personal preferences on others (smoking, religion, zoning, etc.), there is the viable alternative of 'voluntary negotiation.' This means you (or a group you form) approach the bar owners, or your neighbors, and try to make a deal that serves your wants and needs. Bar owners want customers; maybe they will create a non-smoking room. This applies to any situation. It is peaceful and proper, and no 'tyranny of the majority' is employed.

j) The government cannot do things that are illegal or immoral if done by citizens. Sadly, unethical practices (which should be illegal) such as 'progressive' taxation ('tax the rich' at a higher rate) are justified as 'needed' and a method of charging 'fair share', while in fact it is simply 'gang-theft-by-vote'. Why not have the government rob banks, or give guns to the Red Cross and United Way, for fund raising? This violation of rights is 'tyranny of the majority' and cannot be justified because it is 'the will of the people', 'the American way', and done by the government. There are many other examples (military draft, subsidies, legislative favors, etc.).

The maze of 'social engineering' laws that tell us how to live and work do much more harm than good when all the side effects (unintended consequences) are
considered. My approach emphasizes liberty, personal responsibility, and limited government, which is consistent with our American heritage and Constitution, and history shows it results in maximum liberty, peace, prosperity, ethics, and justice.
Look at the conditions in countries around the world with 'big government' (Progressive, Socialism, or Dictatorships) and judge for yourself. Start with N. Korea, Cuba, and the several '.xxstans' (former Soviet Republics).

3. Debt, Taxes and Spending:

These demons of government abuse all tie together! One needs, or feeds, the other. The citizens lose. See my **'Restore Peace and Prosperity'** plan in Chapter 4 for more details.

A. Debt: Domestic and foreign debts are at record levels, for both persons and businesses. With a 'national' (or 'public') debt of over $18 trillion, the U.S. government is the world's biggest debtor (and this doesn't count the over $98 trillions of unfunded Social Security, Medicare, and other pension and benefit obligations; see Table 1). Former Chairman Greenspan of the Federal Reserve Bank (Fed) kept interest rates artificially low (not market-driven) from 2000 to 2006 so mortgages were cheap, to 'stimulate' the economy. It is just like taking heroin, and has withdrawal pains when the economy gets 'sick' from mal-investment (too much money chasing deals). People and business borrowed and spent too much of this cheap money, and then the Fed changed policy, so in 2008 we got; 1. A credit 'crunch' (banks have less money to loan), and 2. Increased interest rates that drove-up ARM (adjustable rate) mortgages. This is what caused foreclosures as home 'owners' couldn't meet their increased payments. Alan Greenspan (Fed Chm. from 1987 to 2006) knew he was creating this monster, but did it to keep his job by pleasing his political bosses. I say he should be indicted for malfeasance and fraud! Instead, he is treated like a sage by his accomplices in Congress and Think Tanks. Ben Bernanke (Fed Chm. from 2006 to present) has used 'Quantitative Easing' (Fed-speak for flooding the economy with new money) called QE-1, 2, and 3-Forever as a 'stimulus', but as any Austrian (see Glossary) economist would predict, it isn't working!

The money we send abroad to buy imports comes back to buy government debt or U.S. assets (Treasury Notes, T-Bills, golf courses, part of Morgan-Stanley, etc.), but that can't go on forever. **The US Dollar (USD) is at risk of collapse due to excess creation of new money by the Fed (called 'monetary inflation', an increase in the money supply, like a balloon; which reduces the purchasing power of all USD).**

B. Taxes: Taxes divert money to the government so people and firms can't use it to spend or invest. History shows that the government uses it unwisely, so the economy and standard of living suffer. We must reduce taxes and spending of all types, and abolish most taxes. I **say start by cutting tax rates by 50% or more (the Laffer Curve says revenues might drop less)**. I recommend; a) 'user fees' (school tuition –at least partial-, toll roads, some 'public services', etc.) whenever feasible, b) a low, flat, personal and business income tax (about 15%, reduce over time, with no deductions), and c) a personal 'sales' tax (Not a 'Value Added Tax, VAT, which hides the layers involved), to replace these taxes;'1) variable percent of income (personal and business),2) property, and interest, 3) capital gains, and 4) inheritance taxes. All of these taxes amount to a **'penalty on success'** and targeted **'gang-theft-by-vote'**, plus a double-tax for inheritance. The sales tax is non-intrusive to personal affairs, less 'progressive' (zero or less 'penalty on success'; except that big spenders pay more), has no disincentive to work and earn, and is easy to manage. Liberals-Progressives like to tax 'the rich' to make them pay their 'fair share', but purposely ignore that the top 10 percent of income earners pay about 70 percent of all federal income taxes though they earn only 43 percent of all income. Isn't that enough?? Again, see item 'g)' States Rights on p. 141.

C. Spending
The U.S. economy and dollar are in trouble, and while our DC 'Leaders' are very worried about it, but won't admit it to us regular folks. They start wars to gain control of oil and other nations instead. **Federal spending is out of control.** All the elected folks in DC are on a 'feel-good', 'vote-for-me' binge of unconstitutional and excess projects including wars, empire building, pork-barrel earmarks, welfare, subsidies, and projects that should be handled by States, or eliminated. I say; **'Cut spending by 50%, or more. All projects must be strictly Constitutional (no 'implied powers' or a health plan approved because 'it is a tax', etc.!!**

4. 9/11 and the War on Terror

The facts and logic (means and motive) related to the 9/11 tragedy build a strong case that it was planned by USA and Israeli leaders to create justification for the forever 'War on Terror' and our invasions of Afghanistan and Iraq (for starters). Never forget that; 1) 15 of the 19 bombers who planned and executed 9/11 were Saudis, and 2) A group of Saudi Royals were allowed to fly out of the US on Sep. 12 even though there was a stop on all flights. **Why didn't we invade Saudi Arabia and do a 'regime change' on the despotic royal family? (Hint: We already had a good oil deal with them).** The Saudi Royals, old family friends of the Bushes, are hated by their people, and have paid-off their dominant Wahhabi clerics (a militant sect of Islam and operators of radical anti-American/Christian/Jew mosques and Madrasah schools worldwide; these are the guys who like to lash women because they have been raped) with oil money over the years to avoid a revolution. **Ignoring Saudi Arabia is your first clue that Bush and his team had a hidden agenda for the War on Terror!**

Many well informed, well educated, and sincere people have concluded that **the government at least 'facilitated' the 9/11 attack** as a 'trigger' for their plans to invade Iraq and expand 'Empire-USA'. Israeli and DC both wanted an excuse to invade Iraq and Iran. How else does one explain the series of events such as; 1) FBI inputs on pilot training by Arabs were ignored, 2) NORAD planes were not launched, 3) The towers and building 7 fell straight down at free-fall speed (this can only happen by controlled demolition !), plus the towers were a 'tube' design with large vertical exterior I-beams as the main structure. These beams were cut (severed!) at each floor as the towers fell; HOW??, 4) A demolition company was at the tower site the next morning to haul away debris to a restricted site, then ship it overseas for scrap. (this prevented analysis of how the tower exterior I-beams were cut, and was a massive violation of the crime scene), and 5) the debris and damage at the Pentagon were more consistent with a missile than an airliner crash. The list of suspicious events goes on and on. A further dimension is that the WTC owner, L. Silverstein, faced a huge expense in ridding the towers of asbestos, and had put a big insurance policy on the buildings (with an extra-cost terrorist clause) a few months before 9/11. For more info, see www.scholarsfor9/11truth.org, and Dr. Paul Craig Roberts

Sep-2011 article:
www.globalresearch.ca/index.php?context=va&aid=26520.
The case is not closed!! The 'official' 9/11 report is full of
errors, bias, poor research, and voids. Calling the citizen
investigators 'kooks' working on 'conspiracy theories' will
not stop discovery of the truth. **This contrived justification
for the disastrous War on Terror must be exposed so
that the War can be stopped.**

**If you find it hard to believe that our leaders would lie
to start a war**, and allow our troops to be killed and
maimed for political and economic reasons (not for
defense), then review my essay **'Wars, and The Lies that
Start Them'** (published on Sep-2007) in Appendix 1.
The Bush team of 'neocons' (former Liberals such as
Wolfowitz, Perle, Kristol, Abrams, and Feith who became
'new conservatives' to seek their personal goals; for more
information reference the article "My Alma Mater is a Moral
Cesspool" on the Counterpunch.org website) took
advantage of the atmosphere of crisis generated by 9/11 to
create the 'War on Terror' as a general-purpose, and
forever, project to implement their plan to use force to gain
control of oil and politics worldwide. The result has been an
immoral, illegal and counterproductive crusade. The
documented information below traces how Bush and his
team got us into this mess and why it will be costly, or
impossible, to correct it. All information is verifiable from
multiple sources.

**The purpose of Clinton's Balkans war was; 1. To gain
control of the Balkans region so we could build oil
pipelines through it, 2. Build huge Camp Bondsteel as
a regional supply center and airbase, and 3. To evict
China from Eastern Europe** and its oil, including the
Caspian area. Remember the 'accidental' bombing of the
Chinese embassy in Belgrade? Why was NATO involved
when no NATO member had been attacked? **Bush's
invasion and occupation of Afghanistan was primarily
to get access to build an oil/gas pipeline** from

Turkmenistan and Uzbekistan to a warm water port near Karachi, Pakistan (the same reason the Russians invaded in the 1980's; Google 'Afghanistan, Unocal'). This project had been delayed for many years but was suddenly approved in Dec-2001.

On June 22, 2008, Eric Margolis, Mid East expert, and former Toronto Sun journalist (ericmargolis.com), issued the article: **'These wars are about Oil, not Democracy'** which tied together the various political, economic, and oil/gas issues as follows (excerpts): *"PARIS -- The ugly truth behind the Iraq and Afghanistan wars finally has emerged. Four major western oil companies, Exxon Mobil, Shell, BP and Total are about to sign U.S.-brokered no-bid contracts to begin exploiting Iraq's oil fields. Saddam Hussein had kicked these firms out three decades ago when he nationalized Iraq's oil industry. The U.S.-installed Baghdad regime is welcoming them back. Iraq is getting back the same oil companies that used to exploit it when it was a British colony.*

As former Fed chairman Alan Greenspan recently admitted, the Iraq war was all about oil. The invasion was about SUV's, not democracy.

Afghanistan just signed a major deal to launch a long-planned, 1,680-km pipeline project expected to cost $8 billion. If completed, the Turkmenistan-Afghanistan-Pakistan-India pipeline (TAPI) will export gas and later oil from the Caspian basin (Turkmenistan) to Pakistan's Arabian Sea coast where tankers will transport it to the West.

The Caspian basin located under the Central Asian states of Turkmenistan, Uzbekistan and Kazakkstan, holds an estimated 300 trillion cubic feet of gas and 100-200 billion barrels of oil. Securing the world's last remaining known energy El Dorado is a strategic priority for the western powers.

But there are only two practical ways to get gas and oil out of land-locked Central Asia to the sea: Through Iran, or through Afghanistan to Pakistan. Iran is taboo for Washington. That leaves Pakistan, but to get there, the planned pipeline must cross western Afghanistan, including the cities of Herat and Kandahar.

PIPELINE DEAL: In 1998, the Afghan anti-Communist movement Taliban and a western oil consortium led by the U.S. firm Unocal signed a major pipeline deal. Unocal lavished money and attention on the Taliban, flew a senior delegation to Texas, and hired a minor Afghan official, Hamid Karzai.

*Enter Osama bin Laden. He advised the unworldly Taliban leaders to reject the U.S. deal and got them to accept a better offer from an Argentine consortium. Washington was furious and, according to some accounts, threatened the Taliban with war. **In early 2001, six or seven months before 9/11, Washington made the decision to invade Afghanistan, overthrow the Taliban, and install a client regime that would build the energy pipelines**. But Washington still kept sending money to the Taliban until four months before 9/11 in an effort to keep it "on side" for possible use in a war against China.*

***The 9/11 attacks, about which the Taliban knew nothing, supplied the pretext to invade Afghanistan**. The initial U.S. operation had the legitimate objective of wiping out Osama bin Laden's al-Qaida. But after its 300 members fled to Pakistan, the U.S. stayed on, built bases -- which just happened to be adjacent to the planned pipeline route -- and installed former Unocal "consultant" Hamid Karzai as leader.*

Washington disguised its energy geopolitics by claiming the Afghan occupation was to fight "Islamic terrorism," liberate women, build schools and promote democracy. Ironically, the Soviets made exactly the same claims when they occupied Afghanistan from 1979-1989. The Iraq cover story was weapons of mass destruction and democracy.

Work will begin on the TAPI once Taliban forces are cleared from the pipeline route by U.S., Canadian and NATO forces. As American analyst Kevin Phillips writes, the U.S. military and its allies have become an "energy protection force."

Margolis also gave us early warning with his March 2, 2003 article '**Bush's War is Not About Democracy'**, which said, in part: *"Bush's war is not about democracy, weapons of mass destruction, human rights, or terrorism. It has two main motivations. First, the Manifest Destiny crowd in Washington, led by VP Dick Cheney and Defense Secretary Donald Rumsfeld. The terrible events of 9/11 have seemed to produce an almost psychotic reaction in these good, patriotic Americans, transforming them into 19th century imperialists.*

Their intention is perfectly clear: 1) prevent any nation ever challenging U.S. global hegemony; 2) dominate oil. The aggression against Iraq is not about oil per se, it is about control of oil. Before the Iraq crisis, the U.S. imported about $18 billion of crude oil annually from the Mideast, but spent $31 billion keeping military forces there. Why? Control of Mideast oil gives the U.S. domination over Europe and Japan, which draw most of their oil from the region.

Domination of the Mideast and Caspian Sea oil will assure the U.S. a permanent stranglehold over China and India, as well as Europe and Japan.

The second driving force is Israel's far-right Likud government, many of whose ideas have come to dominate Bush administration policy and U.S. media commentary on the Mideast.

The Clinton administration was close to Israel's moderate Labour Party; Bush's camp is totally aligned with Israel's aggressive far right and mirrors its views and policies to a remarkable, unprecedented degree.

*Likud and its powerful American supporters want the U.S. to crush Iraq into pieces. **The principal beneficiary of the war against Iraq will be Israel**.*

ADDED BENEFIT: From Washington's viewpoint, the TAPI deal has the added benefit of scuttling another proposed pipeline project that would have delivered Iranian gas and oil to Pakistan and India.

India's energy needs are expected to triple over the next decade. Delhi, which has its own designs on Afghanistan, is cock-a-hoop over the new pipeline plan.
Russia, by contrast, is grumpy, having hoped to monopolize Central Asian energy exports.

Energy is more important than blood in our modern world. The U.S. is a great power with massive energy needs. Domination of oil is a pillar of America's world power. Let's be realistic. Afghanistan and Iraq are about oil, nothing else."

Too bad the US citizens and Congress didn't pay more attention to Margolis' prescient words.
On May 13, 2009, Pepe Escobar wrote a fine piece tying together all the pipeline activity and war-politics in the greater Mid east with his: **'Pipeline-Istan: Everything You Need to Know About Oil, Gas, Russia, China, Iran, Afghanistan and Obama'** (see

www.alternet.org/story/139983). It shows how oil dominates all the major military and political activity there, including the USA invasions and wars in Iraq and Afghanistan. **This again confirms that the War on Terror is mostly a false-front to justify invading and controlling greater Mid East countries (from the xxstans to N. Africa; Libya, Mali next?) to get their oil.**

Iraq never threatened the US and Saddam was not a cohort of Osama. As stated by former US Treasurer Paul O'Neill, **Bush and his team had been planning to invade Iraq well before 9/11.** Bush fired him for his lack of 'loyalty', as discussed in O'neill's book 'The Price of Loyalty'. For further insight on Iraq, visit the 'A War in Search of a Reason' column by Ivan Eland. Thus, they started building a case for preemptive war by fabricating phony reasons such as WMDs and branded Iraq as a part of 9/11.

In his 'Letter to the American People' in Nov-2002 (see guardian.co.uk/world/2002/nov/24/theobserver), Osama bin Laden stated that his reasons for opposing the USA were; 1) US bases in Saudi Arabia, 2) extreme US support of Israel, 3) bombing of Iraq for ten years, since 1991, and 4) support of the corrupt Saudi royal family and sale of oil at low prices, denominated only in US dollars (a deal made by FDR in 1945, and Nixon in 1970). Here is the Sept. 28, 2001 interview in which bin Laden states his was not involved with the 9/11 attack; ummatpublication.com/2012/11/25/). As shown in the Margolis quote starting on P. 51 above, Osama was our 'friend' until in 1999 he helped Argentina get the pipeline deal through Afghanistan, so became our enemy! By early 2011 we had decided to invade Afghanistan and 'take' the pipeline deal. Hence our quick invasion on Oct. 7, 2001, 26 days after 9/11 ! Such a major military action required many months of planning, so the plans must have been ready!

A study done by Prof. W. Pape at the University of Chicago, and part of his book 'Dying to Win', shows that **the primary reason driving suicide terrorists is opposition to occupying troops in their homeland** (not religion), which we had done for many years in Saudi Arabia. Yet Bush pushes the fabrication that 'they hate our way of life' as a diversion from the truth. On Dec. 30, 2005 Dr. Paul Craig Roberts, Assistant Secretary of Treasury under Reagan, wrote, "Bush claims that his war crimes are justified because they are committed in the name of 'freedom and democracy'. The entire world rejects this excuse. Sooner or later even Bush's remaining Republican supporters will turn away in shame from the dishonor Bush has brought to America." On Jan. 16, 2006, in his excellent essay on how our Executive branch is becoming dictatorial (http://www.lewrockwell.com/roberts/roberts139.html), Dr. Roberts wrote, " It is paradoxical that American democracy is the likely casualty of a "war on terror" that is being justified in the name of the expansion of democracy."

The **TRUE REASONS Bush invaded Iraq are**:
1) Control of oil (a step to control the greater Mid East),
2) Defense of Israel (plus access to water, oil, and more land for them),
3) Land for permanent bases (hence they had no 'exit strategy'; we built a huge embassy, plus four large airbases and many smaller ones), and
4) Defense of the U.S. dollar (Saddam had converted to selling oil in Euros; we reversed that the day after our invasion).

Also, the Christian Right has a religious reason for insuring the special treatment of Israel, since they believe Israel must exist in order to allow the second coming of Christ. Faith-based persons of influence who favor special treatment of Israel in US policy are Bush, Tom DeLay, John Ashcroft and various church leaders from whom Bush wants support.

In Jan-2006 the sabers started rattling to justify bombing Iran, and are getting louder today in Jan-2013. The 'official' reasons may be different, but the Real Reasons will be the same as three of the above for IRAQ (oil, Israel and defense of the US Dollar). Iran has announced plans to sell oil in Euros. Israel bought 100 'bunker-buster' bombs from us in Nov-2004 (just after the election), and is ready to use them.

The vast 'War on Terror' was created primarily as a cover to give U.S. empire builders the authority to increase their control by meddling in the affairs of other nations worldwide (which just creates new enemies), and restrict objections at home. The 'USA Patriot Act' gives the government excess authority, which is easily abused. Under it, even US citizens tend to be viewed by authorities as 'guilty until proven innocent', and are at risk of being secretly spied upon, or arrested, as terror suspects if they criticize government conduct and policies. All these programs continue with no end, or net benefit, in sight.

A better solution is to stop interfering in the internal affairs of other nations so that we don't create enemies. The media and the Pope call for kindness to the refugees now streaming to Europe, but have ignored the fact that **our Mideast wars created the refugees!!**

As noted above, the primary cause of suicide terrorist attacks is the presence of occupying troops. We should withdraw from our immoral, illegal, and counterproductive ventures in Afghan and Iraq, and most of our bases in over 130 countries worldwide. Bush and his team don't want to withdraw from anywhere because they want to control these places, thus control more oil (and deny it to China), and continue building an Empire worldwide. I **believe in strong defense, but not costly and useless wars that can be avoided with no harm to us.**

5. How Oil, War, 9/11, and the US Dollar are Linked Together

There is a cause-and-effect connection between oil, value of the US Dollar, and 9/11. The two huge problems, shown in A. and B. below, were known by the Bush Team when they entered office in Jan-2001. They had a warfare plan to control oil and politics worldwide, but 9/11 gave them cover to get started sooner and bigger.

A. Risk of Collapse of the U.S. Dollar (USD): The value of the USD is now propped-up in part by the fact that most oil sales (to any buyer) are denominated in the USD. The market value (purchasing power) of all fiat currencies (just paper; no gold or silver content or redeemability) depends on the willingness of others to **use it** (market demand), and **hold it** as savings, or for a nation, as foreign exchange reserves (typically in the form of US government bonds). All transactions are part of demand, but oil purchases are one of the largest and most visible. A major shift to use of another currency, such as the Euro, would cause a drop in USD value, and could trigger a panic to get rid of USD holdings (cash, bonds, real estate) by foreign persons and nations to avoid major loss of value (30 to 50 percent, or more). China has already started, and S. Korea has hinted. Japan could be next. These three countries are the biggest holders of USD denominated assets. A USD collapse would cause a major US depression, and affect others worldwide.

**A shift to the Euro (or any other non-USD currency) by other countries for; 1) Oil purchases, 2) Investments (bonds, businesses anywhere, etc.), or
3) Foreign currency reserves, would reduce support for the USD and is a nightmare scenario for the US.**
In Nov-2002 Saddam converted to Euros, which we reversed just after the Mar-2003 invasion. Venezuela is threatening to convert. Iran started its own 'Bourse' trading

exchange in early 2007 to compete with existing US and British exchanges, and trades in multiple currencies, including the USD, Euro, and Yen. The shift to Euros puts these countries on top of the list for intervention by the US. The CIA plot to unseat Venezuela's Pres. Chavez in Apr-2002 didn't work, but he is on notice.

My Solution: The USD is vulnerable because of; 1) Excess expansion of the money supply ('Inflation', to pay government bills), and 2) Excess spending and debt by the government. Reversal of these errors will bring strength.

B. Loss of Oil and Gas Control to Russia, China and India: The oil industry agrees that within about 20 years the earth will reach 'peak oil' production. This means the wells for cheap oil (easy to reach, pump, and refine) will start producing less ('peak oil'). There will be lots of oil left (tar sands, shale, etc.), but it will be very expensive to acquire and refine. The US is competing with other countries (mostly China and India; Russia has its own) for control of the remaining cheap oil. They are traveling the world together to negotiate long term contracts (China announced one with Saudi Arabia in Jan-2006). The U.S. is invading oil producers on false pretenses to gain control. Russia's long dispute/war in Chechnya is mostly about control of oil, gas, and pipelines in the Caspian region where Russia seeks broad control. India and China face oil shortages in the future so they are cooperating in deals to gain control of oil in the MidEast, Africa and SE Asia. This threatens US availability and price of over 80% of the world's proven 'cheap' reserves. **These are key reasons for the US wars in the Balkans, Afghanistan, and Iraq, and threats to Iran**. The stakes could not be higher, including risk of broad and long wars, and economic depression, for all nations involved.

Rather than seeking military and political control of oil-producing nations (a costly and immoral method), the

US should negotiate long-term contracts for supply. Big customers have clout! This approach will also end creating enemies by meddling in the affairs of other countries.

With the Iraq war not going well, Bush collaborated with the former enemy Sunnis (Cheney's Jan-2006 trip around the region) on a deal to reduce the anti-US attacks inside Iraq so the US can declare victory and get out 'with honor'. **Of course the original plan was to stay forever in order to; a) Control Iraq oil, b) Use permanent bases in Iraq to control the Mid East, c) Defend Israel, and d) Keep Iraq oil sales in US Dollars. Bush's failure to capture Osama bin Laden** was no accident. Having him at large helped keep him (and now Obama) as 'War Presidents' so the above issues could be pursued as part of the forever War on Terror. The same applies to onerous checking and restrictions by the TSA on carry-on luggage for air travel, while the checked baggage is barely inspected. This keeps 'the people' on edge about terror, so they will not object to loss of liberties. The illegal and desperate measures (domestic spying, torture, etc.) taken by Bush showed his concern about avoiding new attacks on US soil, which are made even more likely by his ongoing intervention for the above issues in the Mid East. FLASH - The so-called 'Killing of Osama' in May-2011 by a Navy Seal raid was a staged event to boost Obama's popularity. All insiders believe he died from kidney disease years before. The ultra-phony picture of Hillary, Gates and others watching the raid on TV was a bad joke. The quick dumping of the body at sea, and the convenient death of all the Seals in a later accident??, are two of the many other well-documented reasons to show the whole event was fake.

I support a strong defense, and wars entered for valid reasons approved by Congress. **In their effort to solve the above problems and gain power worldwide, I say the Bush Team operated as an Imperial Presidency,**

with excess use of force and secrecy. They are using: 1) foreign aid, intervention, and war in a plan to control the world's politics and oil, and 2) high spending, funded by debt, to pacify the folks at home. The first version of the warfare plan was secretly issued in Sep-2000 by the 'Project for a New American Century' team (PNAC, a DC think tank) which started in 1997. The plan called for increased military force worldwide to promote control of oil and their special-interest politics. When Bush was elected in Nov-2000, many of the authors (including Rumsfeld, Perle, Kagan, Feith, Abrams, and Wolfowitz: Cheney was a cofounder) joined the Bush team. For details, refer to the 25Feb03 essay, 'The Project for the New American Century', by William Pitt and Scott Ritter (former UN Inspector for Iraq weapons). **As shown by the demise of all previous empires in history, this approach never works. It is a path to military, economic, and ethical failure**. Perhaps due to the bad reputation they got from the failed Iraq adventure, the PNAC gang regrouped in May-2009 as 'The Foreign Policy Initiative' (foreignpolicyi.org) to pursue the same war-based policies.

6. American Independence and Sovereignty

The U.S. has become entangled in a host of international agreements and memberships that threaten our sovereignty, and could oblige us to go to war to protect other nations. The UN, NATO, and International Criminal Court (ICC) are old ones, but more recently we have joined GATT, NAFTA, CAFTA, and WTO. A looming (and largely secret) threat is the North American Union (NAU), which some say would essentially merge Mexico and Canada with us (can you say oil?). It involves building a highway from Mexico to Canada, with 'free-wheeling' rights for Mexican trucks and drivers to operate in the U.S. We should withdraw from any deal or orgs that infringe upon the freedom or independence of the USA.

A major threat is the anti-American "Law of the Sea" Treaty (LOST), or UNCLOS, was deferred again in July-2012 due to lack of votes, but the supporters keep trying. The LOST convention's purpose is to benefit Third World countries by fining and punishing the wealth and technological advantages of the industrialized West. The convention would subject our governmental, military and business operations to mandatory dispute resolution. Any disputes would be decided by the U.N. International Tribunal for the Law of the Sea, a 21-member body representing 155 countries envious of American ingenuity and prosperity. The United States would have only one vote with which to protect American investment, and the transfer of sensitive, militarily useful and proprietary private technologies, and forced compliance with the Kyoto Protocol.

The LOST convention would be an open invitation to activist judges to interpret the convention's intentionally vague provisions against our national security and economic interests. In point of fact, were our Senate to approve the LOST convention, the odds are roughly 155 to 1 that the LOST tribunal would vote to cede U.S. claims to the North Pole and its oil riches to the Russians.
U.S. adherence to this treaty would entail history's biggest and most unwarranted voluntary transfer of wealth AND surrender of sovereignty. LOST, which was a product of the Left/Soviet/non-aligned movement agenda of the 1960s and 1970s, created the International Seabed Authority (ISA). ISA is a new supranational organization with unprecedented powers to regulate all 'sea' activity!

7. Restitution and Compensation: 'The **law of restitution** is the law of gains-based recovery. It is to be contrasted with the **law of compensation**, which is the law of loss-based recovery. When a court orders restitution it orders the defendant to give up his gains to the claimant. When a court orders compensation it orders the defendant

to compensate the claimant for his or her loss.' These are both litigation situations. (en.wikipedia.org)

When the government is the claimant and collects a fine from a lawbreaker, the money is usually kept by the government (another money grab!). I suggest that whenever feasible (the victims are living and known), the victims of the crime should receive the money as restitution or compensation, shared in proportion to the damage they suffered.

8. Health Care

Liberals/Progressives/Socialists strive for 'free' government-provided health care as a right. Of course, any health care program is unconstitutional, but that means nothing to most Congresspersons and voters. 'Universal Health Care' is another attempt to get 'the rich', or at least 'someone else', to pay for everything they want. I have lived in Canada and experienced the fact that when doctor's training, and then salaries, are paid by the government, 1. There are fewer doctors per 1,000 citizens, 2. Importation of cheaper foreign-trained doctors increases, and 3. The patient becomes 'more work' rather than a client they want to nurture and keep, and the level of care, caring, and courtesy declines accordingly. Most Canadians value their English roots and view the government akin to 'Mother', thus are patient with her faults, and proud (sometimes with vanity) of their traditions and Royal Family. Many view 'Americans' as relative ruffians, and self-centered , dog-eat-dog predators who don't care for each other. Hence their pride in, and patience with, their health system.

Of course, government budgets are a huge issue as to which and how much services and medicines are available, and to whom (rationing). The medical specialists and equipment for expensive services such as organ transplants are limited, and people wait for years (and sometimes die) waiting. It's the same kind of rationed care you'll find in nations like France and the England, where waiting lists for lifesaving procedures are sometimes years-long, and the death rates from breast and prostate cancer are twice to three times higher than in the United States. You can't see a specialist (ear, eye, skin, etc.) without referral by a family doctor. Old people are sometimes deemed 'not worth it' for expensive treatments and drugs. It has been illegal in Canada to open a private 'for fee' clinic, since that is deemed unfair to those who can't afford it, but that is changing. Canadian health managers now admit that their system is financially 'unsustainable' (same in France and others), and that formerly illegal 'private services' (non-government doctors who charge a fee) and private insurance will be needed to avoid collapse. Some provinces already allow certain private services, and even pay private hospitals to take care of 'public' patients. At the extreme (Russia, etc.), corruption sets in, and doctors and staff demand bribes for access to services.

In the face of all of the above, Liberals keep pushing for 'universal health care', and they have a friend in Obama. His plan will be announced soon, and is expected to cost billions to taxpayers, with 'the rich' and employers targeted for most of the cost. This source of funding is a ripoff, but upsets fewer voters.

The cost of routine care has skyrocketed since Medicare and Medicaid were started. Health-care spending has increased from 5% to 16% of gross domestic product (GDP). Cost of these programs was the major reason, but part of the price increase is due to; 1. Loss of US Dollar value, 2. The 1986 'Emergency Medical Treatment and Labor Act' (EMTALA) rules that hospitals must give the poor free 'exam and stabilization' service in their Emergency Centers (under the extortive threat of losing their Medicare business), and these unpaid bills are added to those who do pay, 3. Excess payments for malpractice lawsuits (reform of our tort laws is needed), and 4. Collusive price-fixing (minimum rates) set by the state-level American Medical Association (AMA) chapters and their member doctors. Further, the AMA prohibits members from advertising their rates (or skills, and track record of results). If a doctor violates the AMA rules, he/she loses their license to practice, or is harassed out of business (no referrals, etc.)! The federal government would normally attack this practice under anti-trust laws for 'collusion in restraint of trade', but the AMA has political influence, and gets a pass, which we all pay for! Also, as technology and medicines improve, people are living longer, so there are more years of illness and expenses, which often require high cost intensive care and thus higher expenses for each illness. Even young and middle-aged people may incur high expenses if costly new technology and medicines are needed. Un-funded federal mandates for free emergency service at hospitals (the Feds demand compliance or threaten to drop the hospital as an 'authorized' Medicare provider; this is an extortionist violation of rights) is often abused by illegal immigrants, or those that choose to not have insurance, and this causes higher per-day rates (to make up for non-payers) for those persons and insurance firms that do pay their bills.

My Position: I suggest a twelve-part plan aimed at getting the government OUT of patient-doctor-hospital control and funding so that positive free-market incentives guide the patients and doctors:

1) Phase-out Medicare and Medicaid as the lower costs of free-market care become available (as described below, and vouchers in item 12), and start with having higher co-pays on Medicare and Medicaid to give incentive to avoid unhealthy life styles and non-essential visits to, and treatments and tests by, the doctor,

2) Reduce costs by greater use of Physician Assistants (PAs) so a doctor's time is not wasted on routine work the assistant can perform (including clinics run by PAs; see Item 9 below),

3) Use the FDA only to determine and disclose possible side-effects and viability of drugs, but not restrict use of them (or their potency) until there are virtually no side-effects: Let doctor judgment and CONSUMER CHOICE rule!,

4) Bring the lower price and higher quality benefits of competition, and consumer choice into health care by busting the medical pricing cartel and allowing doctors to advertise their rates (web sites ads, etc.), training and results records (see Items 2 and 9; the American Medical Assoc.-AMA- prevents this; same as ABA for lawyers) and practice as members of private, non-government sanctioned groups, rather than just the monopoly AMA; OK there are a few Osteopaths too) and state licensing boards, with all required to disclose their training and record of results,

5) Eliminate dependency on insurance provided by employers. This is a holdover from WW2 when labor was scarce, wages were limited by law, and employers used benefits to attract workers. There is no reason employers should be expected, much less required by law, to provide health insurance (see item 12 below), any more than they should provide food or clothing, to employees. It is just another way to avoid raising taxes (same as free EMTALA hospital service above),

6) Reform our tort laws to reduce excess payments for malpractice lawsuits that doctors must add to their fees. Perhaps a special court system for torts is needed (similar to bankruptcy),

7) Repeal laws that, a. Force (mandate) insurance companies to offer a long list of covered issues (let people choose the combination of coverages they want), 'community rating' and 'guaranteed issue', regardless of prexisting conditions, age, etc., and b. Limit operations to a single state. Mandating benefits is like saying to someone in the market for a new car, "If you can't afford a Cadillac loaded with options, you have to walk." The huge price increases for insurance in MA and NY show the counterproductice results of mandates.

8) Make personal payments for health insurance (but not co-pays or non-insured items) fully tax deductible,

9) Make government medical licenses optional, so we can have a wide range of private practices and clinics, staffed by 'alternate medicine' folks, Physician Assistants, retired or part-time MDs, etc., to see patients for minor problems, including issuing prescriptions for medicine. Prices will drop as the AMA cartel gets some much-needed competition.

This new approach will foster more personal responsibility by citizens (less abuse of the system; less smoking and obesity, etc.), and will give us hospitals, clinics and private practice offices offering; 'Type A' (full service, lots of equipment and specialists), Type B (moderate skills and equipment), and Type C (low cost, run by PAs and volunteer MDs, etc.; they refer cases to Type A and B as needed). This will allow people to check-out their prices, skills and record and make a choice !! With price competition, and no 'mandated coverage' plans, prices will drop, and health and access for all will improve.

If you prefer a government-licensed doctor, fine, go to one and pay more. I now hear rumors that the AMA lobby is pushing to require that PAs have a Ph.D. in nursing in order to offer the above services. YUK!; More restriction to protect the incumbent 'Cadillac' system and MDs.

10) Promote creation of private plans, such as: a) Health Savings Accounts (HSAs), funded by the person/owner or employer, which would pay for routine care and insurance for major illness. Deposits would be tax-deductible, and interest on them tax free. Each person would own theirs so no loss if they change jobs or retire, and b) Fixed payment plans (a monthly fee, no government subsidies) run by private clinics, under their own rules, that will take care of all 'basic' illnesses. Both approaches; a) have positive financial incentives for all parties (stingy spending, shop for rates, healthy life style, etc.), b) take the government and insurance companies out of 90% of the sessions with a doctor, and c) subscribers would buy high deductible ($10,000 to $50,000) private insurance for major illnesses. (Note; This is similar to the voucher system in Part 12 below, but privately financed),

11) Make all State and Federal elected officials and employees (in any agency or department) subject to the same health care choices as the citizens. No special plans for health or pensions!!, and

12) To the extent that government stays involved in health care, it should; a) Be run and funded by each State, with zero Federal control and funding, b) The programs should not pay doctors and control prices, but should,
c) Issue quarterly vouchers (useable only for health expenses and insurance) to 'well' citizens and permanent residents (same amount to all), but not to illegal aliens, and let them shop for the privately provided services they need, including both direct payment for routine care and insurance for major illnesses, and d) To help people caught in transition from the old system, issue special vouchers to those with major 'existing conditions' that preclude their purchasing insurance, with payments continuing until the end of their illness, or death. The value of the vouchers would be owned by each person, and could be transferred;

a) to their account in another State if they move, b) as a gift, or by a will upon death, to other qualified people, in any State. Having the programs funded and controlled at the State level has two benefits: a) It cannot be funded by fake money created out of thin air by the Federal Reserve, thus forcing fiscal sanity on the tax-funded program, and b) Having control distributed over fifty states reduces the size of the administrative bureaucracy each citizen must deal with, and makes States compete as to soundness (including sustainable funding) of their program.

To the extent that employers stay involved they can fund a 'health savings account' that the employee would own and spend (similar to a voucher). History at firms such as Whole Foods shows that employees are stingy with their account (save for future needs) and tend to care for themselves better (more diet, exercise, etc., and less smoking, alcohol, drugs, etc.) to avoid medical expenses.

Private charity (including free services by doctors and hospitals; like the old days!) will take care of the poor. This will work because with taxes and fees reduced by the above reforms there will be: a. More donations to charities, and b. Fewer people (about a 90% reduction) who can't afford health care.

In conclusion, note that none of the above suggestions depend on government rules or control of medical fees or practices. It is an ethical plan because all funding is voluntary and does not use mandatory fees, forced purchases of insurance, or coercive taxing (gang-theft-by-vote). Thus it is a fair, responsible, and sustainable plan.

****

For more info on health care plans, see:

1) www.pacificresearch.org. Their CEO, Sally Pipes, is from Canada and knows their problems well,

2) An essay from The Independent Institute:
www.independent.org/publications/tir/article.asp?a=740
3) A collection of articles from The Cato Institute:
www.healthcare.cato.org
4) 'A Four-Step Health-Care Solution' written by Hans-Hermann Hoppe in 1993
(http://mises.org/freemarket_detail.aspx?control=279)
5) A list of essays on health at Downsize DC, a think tank for 'less government':
http://www.downsizedc.org/bySubject/health
6) An analysis of state health programs
'The Lesson of State Health-Care Reforms' on Oct. 6, 2009 by Peter Suderman of www.Reason.com . Go to http://online.wsj.com/article/SB10001424052748703298004574455560453947646

9. Employee Unions: Unions serve a needed function when they protect members from fraud or abuse (long hours, unsafe conditions, etc.) by the employer. However, once these basic goals are met, the union managers usually try to keep or enhance their jobs (more pay and power) by seeking more concessions in the form of ever higher pay, health and pension benefits, work rules that reduce productivity, etc. As union membership declined in the 1980s, union organizers focused on government workers such as teachers, fire and policemen, prison guards, staffers, etc. (see SEIU.org and AFT.org). Refer to Stephen Greenhut's book 'Plunder!, How
Public Employee Unions are Raiding Treasuries, Controlling Our Lives and Bankrupting the Nation'.
As noted in Issue # 10 Pensions below, "In many cases, benefits became excessive when self-serving managers 'gave away the store' to avoid a strike..." Thus, there is self-serving abuse by both employer and union managers that lead to excessive costs that hurt profits and growth of the employer, or cause bankruptcy, both of which cost jobs! The US steel and auto industries are examples.

The solution is; 1) The government should not give or allow special privileges to unions to boost their income and membership (check-off system for dues, forced union membership when hired –union shop-, guaranteed job after strike, 'prevailing wage' laws, minimum wage, etc.), but 2) Should fulfill its proper role of protecting the rights of citizens (see Issue #2, P. 41), including suits by unions due to abuse of workers by employers.

10. Employer Provided Pensions

An employer has the option of offering a pension plan to employees or not. If offered, there should be written disclosure (dated and signed hard copy) of the rules (co-payments, benefits, age and years of service to retire, restitution of equity upon termination of employment or of the plan, disclosure of fund investments, etc.), and whether the rules can be changed or the plan terminated. Just as with an insurance policy, it is the personal responsibility of the prospective employee to read and understand the plan and decide if he/she wants to work there. In recent years many plans have been changed or terminated (sometimes as part of bankruptcy) by firms in financial trouble. The government created the Pension Benefit Guaranty Corp. (PBGC) to protect workers from loss of pensions. Like most government plans it doesn't work very well. Further, it creates the perverse incentive, or 'moral hazard', of temping firms to take advantage of PBBC. The PBGC disclosed in its annual financial report that as of Sept. 30, 05 it had $56.5 billion in assets to cover $79.2 billion in pension liabilities. There has been an explosion in recent years in the number of big, ailing companies - especially in labor-heavy industries like airlines and steel - transferring their pension liabilities to the PBGC. With billions of dollars flying out of the agency's door, concern has been mounting over its financial footing. In many cases, benefits became excessive when self-serving managers 'gave away the store' to avoid a strike that would; 1) In the private sector, cause loss of profits that would hurt their next bonus, and

2) In government, cause loss of campaign donations and votes. Steve Greenhut tells the story in his book, 'Plunder! How Public Employee Unions Are Raiding Treasuries, Controlling Our Lives And Bankrupting The Nation!' (more at SEIU.org)

My Position: A company need not offer a pension plan, but if it does, the rules must be published when an employee joins, and not changed without negotiation. Anything less would be fraud, and breach of contract. The government's only role should be to require full disclosure of the rules noted above, and ongoing disclosure to confirm that the plan is properly funded. The absence of these two forms of disclosure is what has led to the painful loss of pensions by many employees.

11. Social Security

This was 20% of the FY 2011 Federal budget (started Oct-2010), thus $727 bn, and growing yearly. The present system is a welfare program for seniors, paid to them by current workers. Seniors have no equity (ownership) of the amounts they have paid-in to FICA in their working years (and contributions by their employers) and the government can stop paybacks (checks from the government) to seniors at any time. It is a devious plan and must be reformed before it fails (goes broke due to more recipients than payers) and hurts many people who are planning for it, or already dependent on it. My transition plan is to; 1) Keep the present plan in force for people age 55 or older, make paybacks proportional to amounts paid in (now immigrants get nearly full pay, with a low history of pay-ins), extend start date of payback to age 70, and grant equity ownership for pay-ins made, 2) Reduce payback amounts as needed (due to reduced program income), with five years advance notice, 3) End 'contributions' by employers, and 4) Allow people age 18 to 55 to join the new plan or go 'on their own'. Either way, they will get credit/payment for their prior pay-ins, and interest.

The current program is immoral because it depends on robbing the younger generation for 'contributions' (pay-ins) sent directly to current 'recipients' of paybacks (there is no 'fund', just bonds, –IOUs-), and is unsustainable because costs are rising while 'contributors' are declining in number and income.

My proposed new program below, 'Redick's Private Pension Plan', is similar to the plan in Chile since the hugely successful new version started in 1981 (see; http://www.cato.org/pubs/policy_report/pr-ja-jp.html, by José Piñera, who as Chile's Minister of Labor privatized the state pension system, is President of the International Center for Pension Reform and co-chairman of the Cato Institute's 'Project on Social Security Privatization'; Cato.org). My Plan is optional (individuals join if they wish) where citizen contributions would be invested by private investment fund firms chosen by the citizen, and the citizen would own the account equity. Growth in value would be tax free. A government regulatory body would set some broad investment diversification rules, to avoid high-risk or politicized investments by the fund managers. The contribution amount (weekly or monthly; a percent of pretax pay, or other personal funds) would be chosen by the citizen based on his choice of retirement age. This would encourage middle-class and low income people to start an account, which they would normally view as 'only for the rich'. This program has proven very popular in Chile (90% of workers joined!) due to the ownership aspect, which fosters personal responsibility. There are many side benefits such as increasing capital available for investment (by the pension fund firms) which reduces unemployment, plus better social and economic conditions in Chile. Go to the Cato.org link above for more details.

The 'private' and 'personal' aspects of my Plan will lead to more personal responsibility in our society, including more work, saving and good relations with the family and friends who will help care for the aged. Poverty cases can be served by private charity. The attitude of 'the government owes us everything' and 'it's OK to take others people's money to pay for my benefits' will fade. Thus, my plan is both moral and sustainable.

12. States Rights (Federalism):

The 'Articles of Confederation' were considered too weak on national defense and other matters, so a convention was called to strengthen them. This evolved to writing an entire new Constitution, which was completed in 1787. At first the States were sovereign and dominate and the new nation was referred to as 'These United States'. This soon evolved to 'The United States of America' and States Rights kept getting weaker, especially when the federal government got control of the monetary system in 1913 with creation of the Federal Reserve System (more below). Our constitution grants enumerated powers (a list; if it's not there, you can't do it) to the Federal government (hereafter 'DC'), and by the 10th amendment, all other powers to the States, or people. Over the years, Congress, the President and courts have twisted the 'general welfare' and 'commerce' clauses of the Constitution, and invented the 'implied powers' concept, to grant enormous powers to DC, including overriding existing state laws. The Founders knew it was good to have differences between states so citizens could 'vote with their feet' if laws and taxes got oppressive. This is why U.S. Senators were to be appointed by their state legislatures, so they would better represent the interests of the states in DC (ended by the 17 th Amendment). Part of the reason the DC involvement has grown is that they control the monetary system (run by the Federal Reserve Bank, 'Fed') and, since leaving the gold standard in 1971, can create money out of thin air! The size of the DC piggy bank is only limited by politics in the short run, and hyperinflation and bankruptcy in the long term, and this why states become dependent on DC money for education, health, police, and many other functions normally paid by the people or state. Most state politicians love getting this money, and Congressmen love taking credit for them (it's called 'pork' to get votes and campaign donations), but it comes with strings attached ('You must do X or we will stop sending money for Y'). Thus, DC feels free to impose unfunded mandates such as free emergency health care, and immigrants/refugees, on the states, and activate the National Guard (originally State Militia), without the Governor's permission. Now the Dept. of Homeland Security is sending equipment and money to local police so they can do their dirty work. The police love the new money and power!

My position: Federal power and spending must be pushed back. The Fed's have no business in education, overriding state laws, drugs, abortion, police, and a long list of other state and local issues ! The Federal government should not be involved in an issue, unless empowered by the Constitution. See Issues 29 and 30 below for my positions on Nullification and Secession, and the 'States Rights' essay in Appendix 2, item 'g)' on p. 141.

13. Privacy and Personal Liberty

A. National ID Card: Support for a national ID card (with the same info imbedded in drivers licenses) is growing and must be stopped. Abuse is inevitable in this type of federal system.

B. Wiretapping: Tell your representative to protect Fourth Amendment guarantees against warrantless searches:

Repeal the Protect America Act. The PAA legalizes warrantless wiretapping of U.S. residents, which the Bush Administration secretly began in 2001, and violates the Foreign Intelligence Surveillance Act (FISA) and the Fourth Amendment. (**H.R. 3773 and 3782** would repeal the PAA.)

Restore the requirement for individualized warrants for wiretapping of U.S. communications and email. U.S. Intelligence agencies cannot oversee themselves. The judicial branch has a necessary role in preventing abuses of power. (**H.R. 3782** would restore individualized warrants for any wiretap of U.S. calls or emails, whereas **H.R. 3773** would permit the wiretapping of some international calls and emails of Americans without individual warrants.)

No immunity for telecommunications companies that broke the law by permitting the government to conduct surveillance of their customers' phone and email records. Let the public see the text of Congress's bills BEFORE they are passed. Fourth Amendment rights to privacy are among our fundamental and inalienable rights. The specific text of any bill that may affect these rights must go before the American people for comment.

14. Separation of Church and State

Persons of faith sometimes complain that their right to engage in religious activities is unfairly restricted. They say our Founders were Christians, so the USA is a Christian nation. Well, they were also white males; does that make us a white male nation? Solutions are usually sought in the 'Establishment Clause' of the First Amendment, or 'Freedom of Speech'. I say this is the wrong approach since these clauses are only about the government; 1) Not naming and supporting a certain religion (as had been done in Europe and some states), and 2) 'The free exercise' of the religion chosen by an individual. As shown in 'Dave's Core Principle' (item 2 above), property rights need to be superior to personal rights (such as religion) to avoid conflicts. This applies to many subjects and situations.

My position: I recommend a property rights approach. While it is compulsory to abide by the laws of the government where you live, religion is an optional and personal choice of each individual. Laws and rights of others must not be violated in the practice of religion. Our constitution protects us from tyranny of the majority. Thus, religious groups should not attempt to mix government and religion, even when in a majority (or active minority), since it imposes (by force of law for coins, pledge), or insertion into government events and places, owned by all (schools, buildings, prayers at events) their option on others. The U.S. has complete freedom of religion so people can engage in their religion as much as they like **on their own time, events, and property.** However, just as it would be trespassing for a preacher to enter a private home or event to conduct a service, no religious group can use or adorn property, objects, procedures, or events owned in part by others (such as the government) without the permission of ALL owners (not just a majority), or their authorized agent. This applies to coins, the Pledge of Allegiance, public schools, non-church meetings, displays in government buildings, prayers at public meetings, even if attendance to such events or displays is optional.

A similar issue of trespassing would apply to Islamic mosques using loudspeakers for 'call to prayers' if they create unwanted noise in the neighborhood. The noise should be stopped on the basis of violating the neighbor's property rights ('quiet enjoyment' laws and precedents). Bush-43's 'faith based' subsidies to religious groups are an obvious unconstitutional ploy to promote religion, and should be stopped. Further, it harms religious work by making such groups dependent on government handouts, and subject to its rules (strings attached).

Religion obviously should not be part of our relations with other countries as to special treatment abroad, or with their lobbies in the U.S. (can you say Israel and AIPAC?).

15. Education

Today's K-12 government schools offer essentially only one flavor of education. In some districts parents can choose a school, but this offers minimal variation. They all preach 'government approved' mush that promotes government as the source of 'good and nice' things, and hide the many lies, and unconstitutional, criminal acts of the government, at all levels. Administrators have a perverse incentive to promote poorly educated kids to keep them enrolled so the state and federal money keeps coming. Our students test lower than students in European and Asian schools under similar circumstances. A big part of the difference is the poor work ethic we engender in our kids due to lack of discipline, including almost no risk of expulsion for causing trouble.

My position: Education of children is the responsibility of parents as to amount and type. The same benefits we enjoy from a free market in food, cars, etc. (as to variety of types, and cost) would apply if schools were all private (for profit or non-). By paying tuition, parents would instantly 'be involved' to be sure they were getting their money's worth. School administrators would treat students and parents as customers who seek a good service, and can shop around for it! Good teachers would get raises the same way an engineer does (ask if you feel you deserve it, or quit and go to a competitor). They now risk loss of accrued pension benefits, but this would not apply under my plan in item 10 above. Good teachers attract customers. Parents would monitor curriculum content and teacher quality and negotiate for changes, or leave. Poor quality schools would be exposed by independent testing services or college entrance exams. This would reduce incentive for administrators to engage in grade inflation, because they would get caught.
I say we should, 1) Allow creation of private nonprofit schools without government license or controls (except fraud, a proper government issue), 2) Phase-out property taxes as a source of revenue for government schools

(payments have no relationship to having kids in school), and replace with tuition, 3) Terminate the federal 'No Child Left Behind' program as too costly, mostly counterproductive, and an unconstitutional violation of states rights, 4) Eliminate the federal Dept. of Education, and 5) Write tax laws that encourage donors to create scholarships and endowments to provide affordable access to these private nonprofit schools for needy students. All these changes will allow parents to choose the school that best fits their children's needs (including religion) instead of pouring more tax dollars into the present failing system. 'Do-gooders' will complain that the above approach does not guarantee a certain level (to 9th or 12th grade?) for every child due to negligent or poor parents. They prefer equal mediocrity for all. However, history shows that incentive, parents, and liberty produce much better results than government schools, while private charity helps those in need.

16. Environment

It is important to not cause excess pollution, erosion, floods, noise, odors, or other changes to the natural state that creates hazards or violate property rights, or threats thereto. Remember, your property not only includes land, buildings, cars, etc., but also your body, thus health hazards are included.

My position: Most problems can be handled from a property rights perspective by suing the source for restitution (not just a fine paid to the government). For example, toxic smoke, underground or surface liquid toxics that enter your body, land or other property can be litigated as property damage. Nuisance items such as odors and noise that come upon your property are the same. For non-owned items such as wild animals, protective legislation can be passed, but it is important to not violate other property and personal rights (such as farmers) in the process.

17. Immigration, and Border Security

Problems: Having a 'Work Permit' (green card), becoming a 'permanent resident' or citizen of the US is a privilege that should include a set of rules and obligations. You must apply, be accepted, and follow the rules, or don't come. Our country was built by immigrants who came here to work, be free, adopt the USA as their new homeland, and become Americans (use our language and laws), and that is still desirable. But now, in addition to jobs and freedom, free health, education and other benefits are part of the attraction, and most immigrants (legal and illegal) have no intention of assimilating as Americans. Many citizens, legislators, and foreign governments, want to use immigration as a 'social refuge system' which allows the poor and displaced of other nations to come here and be taken care of (welfare, etc.), rather than work to cure the problems in their homeland. Thus, the Federal government deposits hundreds of Somalis, Hmong, Russian Jews, etc. in communities, without permission of the State government or community. More federal unfunded mandates, arrogance and loss of States Rights! **Thus the US has become a 'salad bowl' instead of a 'melting pot' and many immigrants become a burden on our benefits system.** They often replace citizens working in low-paying jobs, adding to welfare costs and cultural stress, especially for blacks. Many unskilled citizens have lost their jobs to illegal immigrants. The 'illegal aliens' (a term often replaced by 'undocumented', as if they are victims or otherwise legal) are a further risk because they bypass checks on health and criminal records.

Illegal aliens take advantage of our freedoms by getting bolder and publicly demanding 'immigrant rights' (in-state tuition to college, health/welfare benefits, free K-12 school, etc.) even though they are trespassers in our land. The Mar-2006 mass demonstrations in many US cities are a good example. They were timed to occur a week before Congress started debate on new laws.

Minimum wage laws are a big part of this problem. Most laws require pay of $7 per hour or more, and many jobs don't justify this pay (i.e., employer can't make a profit), so employers look for other solutions. Cheap immigration labor is one alternative because they will work for cash at under $7 hour (this saves FICA payment for the employer also). It is said that Americans won't take the below minimum wage jobs, so immigrants are needed in order to get unskilled work done. WRONG! Americans will do the work, but **wage laws prevent them being offered** at low rates. If the competitive market doesn't support the prices needed to cover the high minimum wage, the jobs disappear, or are secretly given to illegals. **When displaced by cheap illegal immigrant workers, our unskilled citizens may just go on welfare, leading to cultural problems and higher government expenses. Illegal immigration is not the answer to achieving price reductions!** Most politicians ignore illegal immigration because: 1) cheap labor is sought by their campaign donors, or 2) immigrants are likely to vote for politicians who hand out the free services (in most states it is easy to just get the ID needed to register from a trash bin). Illegal immigration is increasing because of: 1) the ease of walking over the border, 2) the corruption and restrictions that inhibit creation of jobs in their homeland, and 3) lax enforcement by the INS at the border and in the US.

The government of Mexico lobbies against US immigration reform because it wants the $20 billion dollars per year their people in the US send home (known as 'remittances'). After oil, this repatriated money is the second biggest source of income for Mexico.

The Mexican government also encourages illegal immigration because it relieves pressure to reform the government socialism and corruption that reduces job creation in Mexico. Their Ambassador refuses to use the term 'illegal' in reference to those who sneak over the border when interviewed on TV, and they published a booklet to assist illegal entry.

Few people know that Mexico has many restrictions on Americans who live there. Americans cannot own property, or get citizen-style health and education benefits, such as they demand here. **While the Mexican government not only requests, but claims special rights for 'their people' in the U.S., it is a FELONY to be an illegal immigrant in Mexico, subject to fines, imprisonment and deportation. What dishonesty and chutzpa !! What a bizarre one-way deal they are demanding!!**

Our proud and historic tradition as a 'melting pot' is being abused. There are lumps and islands in the pot made of people who are here illegally, or refuse to assimilate.

My Solution: 1) Employers should be required to verify legal status of all current employees and then all new hires, of any ethnic group (hence, there would be no charges of profiling), and have the government ship the illegal persons home. Once the word is out that deporting is being done, many would leave on their own.
2) Border restrictions, and temporary resident permits, should be enforced. Laws against harboring criminals and abetting illegal acts should be enforced. This will stop the work of bleeding-heart liberals and misguided religious folks from encouraging and performing illegal acts.
3) The 14 th Amendment should be revised or interpreted, so 'birthright citizenship' does not apply to children of illegal aliens. Since the loosened rules in the Immigration Act of 1965 a flood of immigrants, then their relatives, have come to the US primarily for jobs, and benefits, and most have no intention of learning English or assimilating (i.e., becoming 'Americans').

4) Proficiency in English should be a requirement for citizenship. The U.S. should adopt English as an official language for all government documents and discussions, including voting info. This will reduce costs, and encourage assimilation. Having public documents (by both business and government) issued in multiple languages, and so-called 'multiculturalism', creates a trend toward cultural disintegration in any country. The 2006 riots in France, Germany, Australia, and England are examples of the results.

5) Immigrants must agree to follow U.S. laws. If you want to live under Islamic 'Sharia', don't come! Religious activity, such as Islamic calls to prayer on loudspeakers which cover a neighborhood, must be treated as a violation of the neighbor's property rights.

6) The concept of 'hyphenated Americans' (such as 'Mexican-, and African-American') should be discouraged (but not made illegal), since it tends to slow assimilation and create separate sub-cultures. This hyphenation is a sign of resistance to assimilation (a desire to keep your group separate). There should be an oath (spoken, written, witnessed, and signed) upon becoming a citizen that the person will adopt the USA as their new homeland, and give it their first loyalty above their religion and former homeland.

7) Enforce the fact that illegal immigrants have no 'rights' except humane treatment while they are being deported! In March-2006 there were huge demonstrations in many U.S. cities by immigrants (legal and illegal) demanding there self-made 'rights' that they claim are about the same as U.S. citizens!

One of the best solutions is to improve the legal immigration process. Excessive delays (years), and rude staff (both are typical problems in government programs), cause many otherwise honest immigrants to sneak in.

18. Private Property and Eminent Domain

Private property rights are the foundation of a just and prosperous nation. History, and the world today, shows that justice and prosperity are reduced by lack of such rights. 'Partial Takings' abound due to down-zoning of property by the government at all levels (Federal to city). An example is when they rule that, to maintain 'open space', a farmer can't lease a patch of his ground along a road to a billboard firm. At the very least, he should be compensated for loss of income, and land value. The examples are legion. **If the 'community' wants open-space, let them pay for it!** The same logic applies for abuse of eminent domain, where 'public use' is applied to taking (owner is forced to sell at an appraised price) someone's home so a business that sells to the 'public' can use the land for a store, condos, etc. Liberals like to take money from 'the rich' using 'gang theft by vote' to fund their projects, so it is only a small step to use eminent domain to take land! I will fight to stop this abuse.

19. Gun Ownership

Activist groups, and politicians seeking votes, have attempted to limit private gun ownership by citing the threat of accidents in the home and killings (single or mass) by crazed or criminal people. **They attempt to eliminate damage by deviates and criminals by restricting everyone**. The Dec-2012 Newton, CT, and more through 2015, killings prompted Pres. Obama and other to seek prohibition, and other restrictions, on a long list of guns.

My Position: The second amendment to the Constitution is usually cited as the legal basis to own a gun, but this is related to state militias (why else mention it). In fact, gun ownership is an inherent right, the same as owning a potentially lethal device such as a car, knife, or ball bat, and **it is only improper use that should be subject to public concern or government regulation**. Concern over gun abuse is more emotional than real. The record shows that 99% of gun-owners are very safety conscious. Since

84

the 1930s the U.S. population has more than doubled, and the number of guns in the US has quintupled, yet firearm accidents have been cut in half. A 2002 study in Maryland shows firearms average 0.8% of unintentional deaths in over the 18-year span. As to hazards to children in the home and family life, the study showed drownings take more lives of children under 14 than firearms by a factor of 18. Even knives, bees, and scissors take more children's lives than firearms. More children suffocate (e.g., choke on solid food, etc.) by a factor of 16 than die from firearms. In some cases in the last ten years, the crazed killer may have been affected by medicines that control depression, anxiety, etc., as discussed in this link http://lewrockwell.com/rappoport/rappoport13.1.html .

Another stimulant for thugs and crazies may be to copy the immoral and illegal 'justified' killings that our government does when they invade nations for political (control) and economic (oil, etc.), often using '9/11' as the reason. Killing becomes viewed by US citizens as 'normal' and 'routine'. Thus, 'Step 1' in reducing the growing attitude that 'violence is an OK way get what you want' should be the end of our wars for Empire-USA (not defense). An early domestic example is the government's counterproductive 'War on Drugs' (started in 1971) which has created drug dealer turf wars that account for over 90% of deaths by guns in the U.S.(see more at #22-Drug War, p. 89 below). Raids on drug makers, dealers, and users were the original justification for local police SWAT (Special Weapons and Tactics) teams. In most cities the team members get extra pay for SWAT work so there is incentive for abuse by using them for routine 'suspected' non-drug crimes, even without a warrant. Use of military vehicles and guns has become popular, especially when given to them by the federal government

As to making killing 'routine', the rapidly increasing use of drones (at home and abroad) make it easier and cheaper (no pilot training or deaths, no expensive cockpit to house them, etc.), and Obama and his military pals don't mind 'collateral' killing of innocent people, and facilities, that drone attacks almost always cause!! Now we hear of local police using drones. All the above issues and facts are ignored by the gun grabbers! In England, Canada, and Australia where gun ownership is highly restricted, burglaries and muggings (even daylight home robberies) have increased because criminals feel safe. The deterrent effect that your target person may have a gun is gone. In states where concealed-carry is allowed, muggings and armed-robberies decrease because criminals are afraid their targets may be armed. The same applies to schools where the principal or a guard may be armed. I say anti-gun activists should focus on real causes and threats and leave responsible gun owners alone.

Remember; **The muggers and killers can get guns no matter what restrictions are put on purchases and 'carry'! They don't care what the law says!! Putting a 'No Guns Allowed' sign on your front door disarms the good guys, and makes you a target for bad guys!!**

20. Social Programs; Welfare and Culture

Our vast social programs, preferred minorities, and uncontrolled immigration, are destroying our culture. We are at the 'tipping point' in many areas where benefit recipients and new (often illegal) immigrants control the vote. Government has become Mother and Boss, and people become dependent and demand handouts and other special treatment as 'rights', rather than working for their own success. Ethics are in decline because one's reputation matters less when a person is shielded by Mother's laws. Law breaking and misconduct thrive.

I want all levels of government to 'back off' and let people manage their own affairs and interaction. Private welfare and counseling (such as Red Cross, Salvation Army, Goodwill, churches, private orgs, etc.) will serve the truly needy well. Further, private groups require less than half as

much money to do the job due to better efficiency, and reduced overhead, fraud and abuse. The end of the 'entitlement' attitude and laws will cause people to manage their lives better. There will be fewer self-made 'victims', and more 'responsible citizens'. Incentives rule !!
Humans thrive in an environment where they are comfortable with the region's personal value system, laws, religious attitudes, etc. This gives the feeling of 'home'. A common language has a lot to do with this bonding.
Today, a high percentage of immigrants (legal and illegal) have no intention of assimilating. They are only here for jobs and benefits. This will lead to strife for all.

History and logic show that my 'less government intervention' approach not only yields more liberty, but more peace, justice, prosperity and better ethics. This approach **rewards personal responsibility and work,** and private charity cares well for the needy (and there are about 80% fewer cases due to reduced abuse, reduced perverse incentives-i.e., 'career' welfare users-, lower costs due to use of volunteers, and no 'entitlements').

The 'more government' systems, **such as pushed by Progressives, Liberals, and Socialists, have the opposite effect**, and do more harm than good (counting side-effects)

When people become dependent on government, they care less about support from, and relationships with, friends and family. **As these relationships whither, other social problems such as crime, broken homes, and laziness grow.**

21. Gay, Ethnic, and Hate Laws

There are many conflicts in the law as to what gays (homosexual persons) can do. Marriage and adoption are active now. Most churches view gay conduct as a sin (i.e., wrong even if you are not violating or threatening another's rights; see issue 2, 'Core Principle' above). Of course, those who consider it a sin (or on any subject; abortion, gambling, etc.) are free to peacefully promote their views, short of violating the rights of the so-called 'sinners', by ;1) Setting an example by their conduct, and 2) Lobbying the government for passage of laws to impose their views on others by force.

I view these conflicts as examples of why the government should 'back off' and abolish laws that control our lives by favors and restrictions (i.e., social engineering). Marriage is a personal matter **and none of the government's business.** Favorable tax laws for married persons should be abolished. A 'marriage contract' will handle inheritance, etc., and should be used by all; gay and straight. Adoption should be controlled by the birth parents and private orgs (if parents died together, gave-up rights, etc.).

Laws giving any group special rights and preferential treatment (which creates a 'preferred minority') should be abolished also. Such laws are easily abused by ethnic persons or groups. For example, 1. In Oct-2007, the former football coach of a major U.S. university won a $2 million judgment claiming the school fired him because of his race (black), not his 6-27 won-loss record, and 2. A minority person now feels free to park illegally (including at the front door!) of a shopping center, or post office, etc., since usually no one will challenge them for fear of a lawsuit, or being attacked! 'Hate Crime' laws are another example. There should be no 'special' penalties; murder is murder. **All citizens should have the same rights, with no special rights or privileges for gays, or any other group, as to race, sex, economic or social status, religion, etc. (see 'Core Principle' in Issue # 2 above).** People should be able to associate with (or avoid) whomever they want without fear of lawsuit for violation of special 'civil rights', and the same applies to clubs, employers, etc. as to membership, hiring, and firing (short of violating a person's legal rights). This approach leads to a just and harmonious society, where people learn to 'get along' without government coercion.

Restrictions and favors do more harm than good as to improving social, and economic success of minority groups. Special rights and subsidies reduce incentive for self-improvement, and create the opportunity to abuse such rights. Intrusion in people's lives is unconstitutional and none of the government's business.

22. The Drug War
Our legal system for drugs is antiquated and distorted with hypocrisy and inconsistencies. 'Drugs' such as nicotine and caffeine (stimulants, uppers) and alcohol (a depressant, downer) are legal to use and available anywhere. They are both damaging to health, but are legal for political reasons (voter demand, campaign contributions), and because the government wants the tax revenue. Other uppers and downers are illegal. Extracts of marijuana with proven medicinal uses are illegal, while morphine (made from otherwise illegal opium) is used by doctors for pain suppression. Why is one OK and not the other? Changes are needed. While excess use of 'sporting' drugs is a serious medical and social problem, only fools and ignorant youths do it. However, I say criminalization of such stupid activity only makes it worse (our experience with alcohol prohibition is a good comparison). Further, such use is none of the government's business unless the user violates or threatens someone else's rights (see Dave's 'Core Principle' in issue # 2 above). The FDA and our 'War on Drugs' do much more harm than good. Users can get drugs easily even after years of the Drug War (but they cost more now), and the violent 'turf wars' of pushers and gangs, plus burglaries and muggings by users to support their habit, are worse than ever (see above # 19, Guns, p. 84). It also corrupts police; 1) With the easy abuse of **'asset forfeiture'**

laws, which police can be impose as 'civil' arrests on just 'suspects'; no profit on illegal acts; they can confiscate – and own – any asset that was 'associated' with a 'suspected' crime. This includes local police taking title to, and selling (their department keeps the money!), cars, boats, planes, ranches, etc. without trial. The owner can sue for return, but this takes time and money and may not work, and 2) By the funding and excitement from SWAT Team 'combat' style attitudes and equipment (see # 19, Guns, above)

My solution is to treat drugs like alcohol and nicotine (tax it and control age of buyer and offer optional control on purity of product), and handle abusers as; a) A mental and medical problem, or b) Illegal if a user threatens others, such as driving a car while high. Abuse and violence will soon subside, just as with alcohol, after the end of prohibition. The fact that many drugs are more potent than alcohol makes it even more urgent to get such business out of the hands of criminals. This approach has worked very well in Portugal, the Netherlands, and some U.S. states (CO leads, with lots of tax revenue as a bonus!)

23. Energy

Problem: Energy costs and consumption are going up worldwide, while oil reserves and production (barrels per day, B/D) are going down. The world's daily production averaged 83 million B/D in 2004, and the USA consumed about 25% of it (with only 4% of the world's population). Production of 'cheap oil' (cheap to find, pump and refine) is forecast to decline to 39 mill. B/D by 2030 while consumption increases to 118 ! This is the 'peak oil' concept, where wells in liquid oil pools start to produce less per day. The difference will have to be made up by coal, natural gas, tar-sands, shale-oil (by 'fracking'), nuclear, wind, solar, and bio-fuel, algae farms, etc., **plus reduced consumption and more CONSERVATION !!** Each fuel has its own economic, technical, and enviro issues. Oil has been cheap to get, and convenient to use, so has been the first choice so far. As the price of oil goes up, these alternate fuels will become more attractive, especially if renewable and/or sustainable.

Consumption by China and India is growing faster than any other country. They are shopping for long-term OIL DEALS, big time! This ties-in with why Bush invaded Afghanistan and Iraq, and Obama is threatening Iran (as I write in Jan-2013); namely to control the Greater Mid East oil producers (including Uzbekistan, other 'xxstans', the Caspian area, and North Africa) before other countries make deals for it. An underlyimg reason is to prevent access by China, thus limiting their growth. USA leaders want it ALL!

Solution: I recommend; 1. End the Afghanistan and Iraq wars, and engage in peaceful oil-supply negotiations with all producers worldwide (we are a big customer, and they need us!), 2. Allow eco-friendly oil drilling in all parts of the USA. Note that the Audubon Society has done this in their preserves, 3. Encourage development of alternate fuels and methods (such as electricity from new-generation engines, solar, hydro and nuclear, but no subsidies), and 4. Allow gas and oil prices to rise to their free-market levels, without subsidies or control, but with appropriate anti-pollution laws based on property-rights (of your body, water, air, and land) for those people and places at present or future risk. The past errors, distortions and fears of nuclear energy need to be updated and corrected so the new and safe methods for generation of electricity can be employed. Safer thorium could replace uranium.
　These four changes will give incentive for conservation and production of alternate energy. The free market is very good at responding to demand. Government bureaucrats always spend more and accomplish less than people using their own money, and their projects usually do more harm than good. For example, consider the politically-driven scandal of subsidies for ethanol, which is toxic, expensive,

causes land misuse by excess corn production, is bad for the environment, and increases food prices, etc. BOO ! Algea farms, using flooded ponds, have good potential because they; use minimal fertilizer; can use areas with bad soil; and can use saltwater. New 'external combustion' engines are more efficient, and can burn low grade fuels. For a comprehensive list of energy choices, see www.peswiki.com.

24. Traits of Capitalism and Corporations

Liberals, Socialists, and Progressives like to attack 'Capitalism' and label it as a 'social system', and 'corporations' as bastions of greed and abuse. However, Capitalism is properly defined in my 1953 and 1961 dictionaries as **an 'economic system'** based on private ownership and free enterprise. It is also a moral system because all conduct is voluntary. Current dictionaries have crept toward defining it as a 'social system' as Liberal editors take control; very convenient, but false. A Corporation is just a legal structure to allow shared ownership and financing. Liberals like to say that corps are a way to avoid personal responsibility. These definitions were invented by Liberals as straw men to avoid their own complicity in corrupt and unconstitutional government. It is bad 'people' (as usual; same for churches and governments), bad laws, corrupt government (including legal 'favors', subsidies, etc.), and perverse incentives that cause the trouble. Liberals avoid criticizing government because they want it to keep giving the legal favors and welfare, **but only to their projects**. What a pile of ignorance and hypocrisy! For example, the June 26, 2002 main editorial in the Wall Street Journal, by Dr. Henry Manne (George Mason Univ., Univ. of Chicago, etc.), made a great point that the Williams Act of 1968 (now rules 13d and 14d of the 1934 Securities Act) was the birth of the Boardroom and Officer fraud and self-dealing we have been seeing since the '80s (it took a few years to set in). The new law required takeover groups to announce their intent once they had 5 % of the target stock, which gave warning so officers could protect themselves. This allowed officers of many firms to get lazy and corrupt without risk of getting booted-out. Remember, corporations become takeover targets only because their profits, and return on assets, are low, usually due to bad management. In takeovers, the shareholders win, but bad managers lose! Thus, at-risk bad managers whine to the government for protection (can you say 'campaign donation'?). Many states have passed laws to 'protect' their local firms from 'outsiders', and the 'poison pill' was born to fend-off the takeover groups! Another factor is the shareholder laziness that developed in the 1990s as stock prices soared due to inflation. The attitude was 'all's well', 'no worries'. It wasn't long (and quite predictable) that the nomination of Directors by shareholders was restricted, and biased 'Buddy' Directors were selected by Officers (a 'slate'). The self-dealing started, and the combined 'Chairman and CEO' position was born (an inherent conflict) ! These hot-shot CEOs plundered their firms with huge salaries and stock options, while trying to set a glorious, resume-enhancing, growth record with short-term, unsustainable, profit enhancements (reduce staff, announce grand plans, etc.), and excess debt, spending and risk They often got themselves and their firms in business or legal trouble, but left with 'golden handshakes' or hung around a while with 'retention bonuses'. There are hundreds of examples! Why should a low-performing, or corrupt, CEO get a multi-million dollar bonus when fired?? It is white-collar theft! The Dodd-Frank bill of July-2010 issued a vast set of rules to correct abuses, but puts a major compliance burden on firms.

Solution: I say the solution is to repeal the Williams Act, and other distortions of the free market, not pass a slew of new regulations. Let the free market do its work, so shareholders will wake-up then nominate and vote for honest, competent Directors that select and monitor the officers.

25. Origins of 2008 Crash and Effect of Bailouts

The rush of home loan defaults and bank problems started in late 2007, and peaked in Sep-2008, and is continuing, but less, at this writing in Jan-2013. The underlying cause was Fake Money, as described in Chapter 3. This excess supply of money, delivered to lenders by the Fed and its pals at FreddieMac and FannieMae, was the 'mother's milk' of market distortion. A trigger was the 4.25% increase (from 1% to 5,25%) in interest set by Greenspan when he ended his Fed term in Jan-2006.

A major facilitator was the Community Reinvestment Act (CRA), a 1977 federal law that requires banks and thrifts to offer credit throughout their entire market area and prohibits them from targeting only wealthier neighborhoods with their services, a practice known as "redlining." The purpose of the CRA is to provide (force?) credit, including home ownership opportunities, to 'underserved' (unqualified?) populations and commercial loans to small businesses. OK, getting their votes may be part of it!

The CRA was passed into law by the U.S. Congress in 1977 as a result of national grassroots pressure for affordable housing, and despite considerable opposition from the mainstream banking community. The CRA mandates that each banking institution be evaluated to determine if it has met the credit needs of its entire community. In 1995, as a result of interest from President Clinton's administration, the implementing regulations for the CRA were strengthened by focusing the financial regulators' attention on institutions' performance in helping to meet community credit needs. These changes were very controversial and as a result, the regulators agreed to revisit the rule after it had been fully implemented for five years. Thus in 2002, the regulators opened up the regulation for review and potential revision.

The Clinton Administration's regulatory revisions with an effective starting date of January 31, 1995 were credited with substantially increasing the number and aggregate amount of loans to small businesses and to low- and moderate-income borrowers for home loans. Part of the increase in home loans was due to increased efficiency and the genesis of lenders, like Countrywide (set up as an 'off brand' by Bank of America), that was aggressive and did not mitigate loan risk with savings deposits (ie, borrowers must have deposits) as did traditional banks using the new subprime authorization. This is known as the secondary market for mortgage loans (high risk for banks). The revisions allowed the securitization (packaging, with insurance, and called AAA; FRAUD!!) of CRA loans containing subprime mortgages. The first public securitization of CRA loans started in 1997 by Bear Stearns, and it helped break them in Sep-2008!. The number of CRA mortgage loans increased by 39 percent between 1993 and 1998, while other loans increased by only 17 percent (a flood of money into high risk).

In the 1980s, groups such as the activists at ACORN ('Association of Community Organizations for Reform Now', www.acorn.org; an Obama favorite!) began pushing charges of "redlining" - claims that banks discriminated against minorities in mortgage lending. In 1989, sympathetic members of Congress got the Home Mortgage Disclosure Act amended to force banks to collect racial data on mortgage applicants; this allowed various studies to be ginned up that seemed to validate the original accusation.

In fact, minority mortgage applications *were* rejected more frequently than other applications - but the overwhelming reason wasn't racial discrimination, but simply that minorities tend to have weaker finances. A study in 1992 proved that bias was not the problem. Yet the harm was done and banks loosened their rules to avoid lawsuits.

A good example is an article on the government's takeover of Chrysler as written by Peter Schiff (see P. 131) on May 5, 2009 and quoted in part here: *"...A real bankruptcy is the only solution. In it, current shareholders get wiped out, current contracts and obligations are voided, which creates the opportunity for new management, with private capital, to scrap out-of-date business practices, and produce cars cheaply and profitably. Under the guise of 'saving jobs', the Administration has disrupted this process."*

Illegally giving control of Chrysler and GM to the UAW and the government in 2009 enshrined a culture of failure and sealed Detroit's fate. Both companies have become government-sponsored entities, not too dissimilar from Amtrak or the Post Office, forever relying on taxpayer funds to create products of dubious quality." Sure enough, Detroit is now full of decay and crime. The police have given-up on serving some neighborhoods!

The statist approach of Obama's 'government intervention and control' will make the economic recovery worse and longer. His re-election in Nov-2012 adds to the potential amount of economic and cultural damage!

26. Occupational and Business Licenses:

Problem: Licenses are touted as a way to protect citizens from faulty or fraudulent services, but in fact usually limit choices to the citizens and give 'cartel or monopoly' status to the license holders. This applies to lawyers, doctors, plumbers, beauticians, restaurants, contractors, etc. where the licensing is often abused by; 1. The government, and incumbent licensees, to restrict new entrants in order to protect themselves and friends from competition, and 2. By associations (unions, medical, legal, etc.) to impose rules such as minimum fees to clients, controlled or no advertising of rates, etc. The government has threatened cancellation of a license to force 'cooperation', such as making phone companies give them private usage data, or radio and TV treat them 'nice'. Another category is when the citizen is subject to, or can be threatened by, the service provider without initiating choice. An example is a truck driver or airline pilot, where one can be run into, or be in a crash, if an unqualified person is providing the service. These should be licensed to PROTECT the citizen, a proper function of government.

Solution: I recommend that licenses be optional when the citizen can initiate choice of the service provider. This would; 1. Allow individuals and firms to offer services, and set and advertise prices, without permission from the government or a 'professional society' or union (let the buyer beware, and decide), 2. Allow groups to form 'professional societies' or unions that set their own standards of quality, disclosure of member skills and performance records, and membership requirements, and advertise them, without government control, and 3. Bring the benefits of competition (better quality, lower prices) to the trade groups (yes, doctors and lawyers are a trade group). Buyers who prefer a government-licensed provider, could use one; but all buyers (patients, clients, etc.) would have a CHOICE of licensed or unlicensed. It follows that the chooser would be responsible for the results and could not sue a vendor for being incompetent if unlicensed.

27. Limits on Terms and Benefits for Congress

Problem: One cause of corruption in DC is that officials will do almost anything to keep their prestigious and profitable jobs (give pork to voters; favors to campaign donors, etc.). Furthermore, they vote themselves pension, health and other benefits that far exceed what they bestow on their constituents. Examples are; a) Better pensions and health care than Social Security and Medicare, b) Their children can include student loan debt in a bankruptcy, c) Any campaign funds existing when they retire belongs to them. Can you say 'Privileged Upper Class'?

Solution: I recommend that: 1. No U.S. Representative may serve more than four terms (8 years), two terms (12 years) for a Senator, or a combined fourteen years if they have worked in both jobs (based on a combined life total), 2. All elected officials get the same pension (Social Security) and health (Medicare) benefits as the 'common' citizens, and with the same rules for calculating fees, and reimbursement of claims, and 3. End any other special treatment that is found.

28. Eliminate 'Earmark' Pork Funding

Most Congresspersons like to 'bring home the pork' to fund state projects and win votes. These 'earmarks' are hidden, unconstitutional, add-ons to other funding bills such as transportation, and 'Omnibus Appropriations Bills' (5 or 10 funding bills combined), and are not discussed in the normal approval process, yet add-up to billions of dollars per year. Even worse, the omnibus bills are usually many hundreds of pages and few Congresspersons read any part of them! Since the government is already 'in the red', this spending is a serious add-on to our national debt problem! I will promote a bill to make earmarks and Omnibus Appropriation Bills (and sneaky 'Minibus' bills) illegal for all Congresspersons. This will eliminate cries by some voters of; 'We're not getting our share of pork'. Of course we will also fight for reductions and elimination of improper grants and subsidies. Unfortunately, in May-2009, Pres. Obama blessed earmarks by saying; 'The local Congressperson knows best what his/her District needs.' Another campaign pledge trashed!

29. Nullification of Federal Laws by States: In

general, nullification is refusal to enforce a law deemed unconstitutional or otherwise illegal. It originates in the concern of government becoming too strong or abusive, and ignoring the Constitution and laws. Key applications are;

1) Refusal of States to enforce Federal laws; State sovereignty over the Federal government is the basis. Recent examples are state nullifications of all, or portions of, the REAL ID Act of 2005, medical marijuana laws, Cap and Trade, and the Second Amendment restrictions

2) Refusal of a jury to enforce charges imposed by a law or the court; This relates to sovereignty of the citizens over all levels of government. On this basis, juries can refuse to impose the penalties decided upon by the court. Over the years, judges and lawyers have made it illegal, confirming the original concern; They want more power!

My position is that nullification is necessary as a check on excess and immoral use of power by the government. Tom Woods Ph.D. explains it well in his book; 'Nullification: How to Resist Federal Tyranny in the 21st Century'.

30. Secession by States from the USA: The USA

was created by secession of the colonies from England. The new 'states' were sovereign entities that created a Federal government, limited in scope by a Constitution. It was a voluntary association that could be ended by the members.

Early examples of 'creeping federal dominance' that violate our freedoms and States Rights were: 1) The Civil War (actually a war of aggression by the North; the South just wanted to leave, not take-over the government) established the Federal government as superior in power to the States based on 'might-is-right', and 2) The Pledge of Allegiance, written in 1892 by Francis Bellamy (a socialist Baptist minister who was fired for his socialist sermons) which included the word 'indivisible'. In 1954, Congress after a campaign by the catholic Knights of Columbus, added the words, 'under God', making the Pledge both a patriotic oath and a public prayer. Both terms are improper because; a) our allegiance should be to the nation (the land and people), not the government, and b) 'under God' violates separation of church and state (inserting religion into a text, place, etc. that is used, and owned, by all).

Recent Federal mandates (Obama's health care, 'No Child Left Behind', TSA, drug laws, etc., etc.) have awakened interest in secession because they violate the Constitution, States Rights, and our fundamental rights of self-government, and voluntary association. Groups in many States have sent secession petitions to the White House! Secession is a proper reaction to abusive and illegal acts by the federal government. As a first step, secession petitions can be a tool to alert Congress and the President to the need for changes. Opponents cite the Article 6 'Supremacy Clause' in the Constitution (which can be argued only applies to laws that are Constitutional). The Swiss use their Referendum process to change laws and terminate the jobs of politicians. We should do the same. In the absence of corrections from DC, full secession can be employed (similar to referendum in #31 below).

31. Constitutional Amendments:
a. Laws by Referendum : The Swiss have been very successful in controlling government abuses and excesses by use of their referendum laws which allow them to; 1) Remove legislators from office (recall), 2) Pass laws that they want but can't get the self-serving legislators to pass, and 3) Repeal laws that they don't like. This keeps the legislators alert to comply with the voter's wishes, and gives voters incentive to be active in managing their

country (rather than whining as 'victims'). I suggest a similar set of rules be invoked, and

b. A Balanced Budget amendment will give us a powerful tool to limit spending. Politicians will like it because they can claim; 'We want to give you more, but our hands are tied!'

32. Abortion

Problem: There will always be abortions. The legality and conditions are what vary. Roe v Wade, and government payments in many cases, have made abortion so cheap and convenient it is often treated as a means of contraception. Carelessness and irresponsibility are rampant.

Solution: I am personally opposed to abortion except to protect the mother's life, and say in no case should the government pay the costs. I further oppose abortion after the first trimester (3 months is plenty of time to make up your mind), and all partial-birth abortions. However, one should not seek laws to force others to comply with one's own value system. Again, The 'Core Principle' applies (see Item 1b above). The question is. 'When does the fetus become a separate person with rights?' Many people take the position that abortion is a moral or religious issue, and assert that 'life begins upon conception' and the fetus is an 'unborn child', just as they righteously assert their dogma about deities, angels, virgin births, Heaven, Hell, etc. in the absence of supporting logic or fact. These are sincere positions, but do not negate the fact that **the fetus is not a separate person with rights until born.** It is a living part of the mother's body, like her arm, but not a 'person' with rights.
As to the law, a woman's body is her property, and does not belong to the government, her doctor, or her church. Thus, it is a woman's right to make an informed choice on what happens to her body. **In fact, for a**

responsible woman there are a series of three choices involved. Whether to;
1) Have sex,
2) Use protection, and if pregnant,
3) Deliver a baby, or have an abortion.
The Roe vs Wade ruling is invalid because the Federal government has no constitutional authority in this area. Thus it is a State issue. In summary:

1. Opponents of abortion should not attempt to impose their personal views or religious beliefs on others by force of law. That would be **immoral and unconstitutional**. They should peacefully oppose abortion without using force or threat to the pregnant woman, or her doctors and staff and their facilities.
2. Proponents should exercise their right without expecting others (including via the government) to pay for it, and they should observe the three choices above.

FLASH: This Jan. 26, 2013 article (//coloradoindependent.com/126827/catholic-schooling) tells us that Jeremy Stodghill, of Canon City, CO, is suing St. Thomas More Hospital there for malpractice in the 2006 death of his wife and twin unborn sons. The hospital lawyers argue that his twin boys, who were seven months in the womb, **don't qualify as people.** ", despite church directives to caregivers to "witness the sanctity of human life from the moment of conception until death" and always to "defend the unborn."   I call this an example of 'situational ethics' , where you change your principles as needed!

33. End of Life Choices: Modern technology allows terminally ill people to live longer, but usually at great expense and suffering (a socially mandated form of torture). To avoid this harm, our laws and societal standards need to be revised as follows. Current law gives four choices for the patient and family; 1. Increasing pain medication (for comfort), 2. Terminal sedation (keep the patient completely unconscious until death occurs), 3. Withdrawing treatments and life-support, and 4. Advance authorization to doctors and family filed by the patient while healthy as a 'living will' and/or 'power of attorney'. Self-inflicted, and patient-approved 'assisted suicide' are illegal (remember Dr. Kervorkian?), but this ignores that in a free society you own your life and body (the government and church don't). It is none of the government's business what you do to yourself, thus should be legal. 'Mercy killing' (no patient approval), is illegal due to possible misuse, but should be made legal with adequate controls (such as family approval when available; always a medical statement that the subjects' comatose is incurable). Moral and religious issues are optional personal choices. Note that the above changes do not grant any legal authority to the government. It is all about personal Liberty.

Blank

Chapter 4: A Plan to Restore Peace and Prosperity

As you read this chapter, please keep in mind this fundamental issue: Our Founders wrote in the preamble, **'We the People … do ordain and establish this Constitution…'.** I say the time has come for We the People to re-ordain and re-establish our Constitution, and **make** our government officials, and judges, comply with it by engaging in a non-violent rebellion. Most (well over 50%) of our laws and spending since 1932 and ALL of our wars since 1776 have been unconstitutional, and started based on lies (see Appendix 1; 'Wars and the Lies that Start Them'). The result has been a serious cultural (more irresponsible and illegal conduct, violence, and corruption by citizens and government) and economic (excessive spending, taxes, and debt) decline in the USA!

 It is time to fight back to restore the rule of law, and stop the abuse and crimes done by self-serving politicians and their corporate and 'more-government, Progressive' friends!

The list of issues in Chapter 3 must be dealt with as part of this plan. Please do your part by choosing a topic there and working to solve it. Owners of this book are authorized to copy pages and send them to their federal or state legislators to urge them to act on my recommendations.

An important goal is to restore traditional American values, principles, and compliance with the Constitution.

I focus on the federal government in DC because it does the most harm with unconstitutional wars, fake money, plus excess spending, taxes, and debt. This is only possible with fake money that is also the world's primary 'reserve currency', since people, firms, and banks, at home and worldwide, will accept it for payment and keep it as a safe

105

'store of value'. Thus, only the USA can pay its bills with an unending supply of newly created money. This feeds the spending, excessive imports (thus 'off shoring of jobs), welfare, pork, wars, and corruption in the USA! It allows DC to impose unconstitutional 'national' laws (on abortion, drugs, free emergency care at hospitals, etc.) that pre-empt state laws and prerogatives, because the State's executives are shameless beggars and must comply or lose some funding. This free ride will end when the world tires of accepting our fake money due to fears our economy is failing. This tragic end of our fake prosperity started with the massive Keynesian-style 'Quantitative Easing' (QE-1, 2, 3-infinity; flood the economy with money!) 'stimulus' programs by the Federal Reserve, started in 2008 and funded by newly created fake money which will eventually result in major price inflation (caused by a major loss of US Dollar value; 50% or more?)!! This approach ignores the need for Supply-Side-style 'investment incentive' tax reductions and low regulation to revive the economy and create new jobs. By 2020 to 2025, the USA is likely to decline, or crash, to a middle-class 'post-empire' nation, operating on a smaller budget. Others who did it are former 'empire nations' such as England, Spain, France, and Russia. Refer to Chapter 2 'Empires'.

One benefit of the USA being cash-poor will be the termination of wars, foreign bases, and foreign 'aid' (bribery) we can no longer afford; A classic case of doing the right thing for the wrong reason.

My plan is shown below. Some of the topics in the plan have been discussed in prior chapters, but the Plan ties them all together.

My Plan to 'Restore Peace and Prosperity': Introduction

The USA is at a tipping point where spending and tax reductions and legal reforms must be made or we will have a more severe economic crash than we have experienced since 2008. Due primarily to increases of our money supply (monetary inflation) to support government spending, the US Dollar (USD) has lost over 95% of its purchasing power since 1913 (when the Fed started), and faces further losses if we don't reduce spending soon. The world views us as a failing empire and other major nations are making preparations to replace our dominance in financial and political matters, including the USD's status as the world's primary 'reserve currency' (any seller or lender will accept and keep it), which allows us to create new money to pay our bills! (and we abuse it!). In 1968, then French President Charles de Gaulle called it our 'exorbitant privilege'. My plan to '**Restore Peace and Prosperity'** shows how we can reduce our arrogant excesses and avoid an economic and political crash.

The Original USA Attitude
Let's look at our nation's history to see how we got into the economic and cultural mess we are in.

The USA has evolved in government and geography in many steps. When the thirteen colonies in America won their independence from England upon signing the 'The Paris Peace Treaty of 1783' on September 3, 1783, they were referred to as '...free sovereign and independent states..' In order to better coordinate their activities and defense, they created the 'Articles of Confederation' on November 15, 1777, then the 'US Constitution' on September 17, 1787, and the USA was born! Both of these documents; 1. Treated the States as sovereign entities, and 2. Were a specific list of limited powers and duties granted to the central government by the States and people. The concept was (and is) that if the power to do or legislate something is not granted therein, the government has no authority to do it, except by amendment.

The settlers came to America seeking freedom and took great care to not grant too much power to their new government. It was viewed as a servant created to only protect the rights of its citizens from violation by others, not to 'manage' the economy or people. Key words are 'protect rights', and 'by others'. Under this legal system you can do whatever you want if you don't violate the equal rights of others (of course 'non-legal' social issues such as honesty, courtesy, etc. still apply). The rights are limited to one's natural rights (such as free speech, property rights, freedom to travel and associate, etc.) that are free and you are born with. They do not include; 1. So called 'legislated rights' (or 'entitlements'), all unconstitutional, that have been created by improper government, and 2. Goals and desires such as health-care, education, housing, jobs, etc. A guide is that 'nothing can be a right if you expect someone else to pay for even part of it'. Sounds good for the start of a new country, but it hasn't worked out as planned!

Personal responsibility was emphasized in early America. Families and private charity, with voluntary donations, took care of the needy. But over time, politicians seeking votes have created 'benefits', 'subsidies', and other favors for people, businesses, and activist groups that have created dependence on the government and have become viewed as 'normal', and 'the American Way' (entitlements). FDR launched the 'paternalistic' style government in 1933 as his solution to the Great Depression, which was caused by excess money from the Fed (see below). Private charity has waned as the government became the source of funding (easier than seeking voluntary contributions).

Since 1782, the governments at all levels (city, county, state, federal) have expanded their role to become a manager, and then controller, of the people and economy, with vast powers to restrict liberty and force compliance to the dictates of politicians, who in turn are often controlled by other groups (corps, unions, activist groups, etc.). The result is that we now have an overbearing government that creates war, debt, and restricts liberty. Police, the TSA and other law enforcement groups often act as aggressors and bosses, rather than helpers to the people. The federal politicians, with their lust for power and endless source of fiat paper money from the Federal Reserve System (the Fed), are the worst violators and cause damage both at home and worldwide.

How the USA Government Grew and the People's Attitude Changed

First, let's look at the major events that enlarged and molded today's USA:

1. 1861, the Civil War; **Postured the federal government as superior to the states.**

2. Wars of aggression to add land and colonies; 1812-'War of 1812'; Attempted to acquire Canada; 1839-'Mexican American War'; Invaded and acquired the northern half of Mexico, now most of the USA SW 6 states; 1898-'The Spanish American War'; invaded and acquired Puerto Rico and Guam, bases in the Philippines, then 'annexed' Hawaii. For details on our wars of aggression, see Appendix 1. Lands acquired by negotiation were; 1803- Rights to French 'Louisiana', 1822-Florida Territory, and 1846-'Washington Territory' by a treaty.

3. 1913, Federal Reserve System; **The Fed; created by and for politicians and bankers to provide a near endless supply of money and credit to serve them.**

4. 1917, US entered WW1 and **became a world power, and the US Dollar a reserve currency** (held by banks, and used for international transactions)

5. 1933, President F. D. Roosevelt launched the Social Security System, the FDIC, ended private ownership of gold, and started many other social and economic programs; **The birth of 'paternalism'.**

6. 1941, US entered WW2, by 1945 became the world's top power, and the US Dollar the world's official reserve

currency (redeemable in gold at $35 ounce, but only between nations); the start of **world domination and Empire-USA.**

7. 1965, President L. B. Johnson **launched Medicare (A & B), and Medicaid**. Now 'others' will help pay your medical bills!

8. 1971, President Nixon ended connection of the USD to gold. Money creation and prices have soared since then; **The start of extreme excessive spending and debt** by the people and government.

The above events created a huge Federal government with worldwide 'interests', all unconstitutional. Now more people work for various levels of government (22.5 mill.) than in all manufacturing (11.5 mill.). This is about the opposite ratio of 1960. (To be fair, the productivity of the average American factory worker has tripled since 1972, so total manufacturing output should not be measured by the number of people employed) **Most people now view government as 'mother' and 'manager'. This creates dependency, careless living, and reduces initiative and personal responsibility**. Immoral gang-theft-by-vote (targeting any person or group that has money) is accepted by most as a normal way to raise money, and is a sign of cultural decay. Our nation has become 'Empire-USA'. Politicians now see the world as their domain, and the 'military-industrial complex' pushes (and bribes Congress) for more foreign wars and occupations to feed their business'. The massive problems we now face is the same as all empires in history that have failed due to; 1. The expense of constant remote wars for control and resources (oil, etc.), and 2. The decline of productivity at home, and demands for benefits (food, housing, health, pensions), by the people. This is the USA we see around us today; A failing empire! For more on empires, see Chapter 2, and Appendix 2.

Details of My Plan to Gain More Peace and Prosperity

This plan shows how to restore control to the people, abolish unconstitutional spending, conduct, and laws (including the Federal Reserve System and undeclared wars), cut taxes, and end abuse of the 'interstate commerce' and 'general welfare' clauses in the Constitution, thus allowing USA citizens to enjoy more liberty, peace, prosperity, morality (more honesty and courtesy, less theft and fraud), and justice. All changes shown below should be made as soon as possible (within 5 years), depending on the size and complexity of the issues. All financial experts agree that a country is in big trouble when its debt exceeds its GDP. The USA debt is 102%. "Progressives' (people who seek more government spending and control to solve social and economic problems) complain that 'cuts' to their projects are cruel, but ignore the greater pain caused by the economic crash that their unsustainable spending and government intervention in the economy has caused. The economic problems since 2008 are just a start. When speaking to these Progressive groups as an election candidate, I have asked if anyone supports 'gang-theft', and none say they do. Yet they all support immoral gang-theft if done by voting to target and tax anyone with money such as 'the rich', 'inheritors', or 'corporations', even if gained honestly and with taxes already paid. This is very convenient compared to soliciting voluntary contributions, but very immoral and counterproductive, and one of the signs of decadence in a failing empire. Of course the business groups (the 'Military-Industrial Complex') and politicians that support invasions, wars, and occupations for economic and political gain (Iraq, Afghan, Libya, etc. for oil and control) for Empire-USA are an equal or bigger part of the moral and economic problem we have.

Due to the Wall Street bailouts in 2008, and the Fed's program of 'Quantitative Easing' (pouring new money into the economy), **the annual rate of debt growth has**

increased faster in the last few years, and is expected to grow even faster in the years ahead!!

Given these dire circumstances, the 'cuts' now planned in Congress do not come even close to avoiding a crash of our economy and the US Dollar.!

The Plan: Parts 1) to 3)

1) Monetary System: (This is a summary of a large topic. For more detail get my 'Monetary Revolution USA', and 'How to Protect and Grow Your Wealth' books at Amazon.com). See essays in Appendix 2.

Key Comment: Remember that the reason our fiat money system is so important in this plan, with the USA as the issuer of the world's primary reserve currency, is that it pays for our invasions, wars, and homeland police-state, **the opposite of our goal for more peace (see; OccupyPeace.us)! We can create new money as needed, and any Seller or Lender will accept it, worldwide!! (but this is declining)**

We now have what is known as a 'fiat' monetary system, where the value of paper money (Fed notes) and coins is the 'face value' declared by the government, and must be accepted for payment in the USA because of 'legal tender' laws. The paper notes are not redeemable in a commodity with market value such as gold, and the coins are made of cheap 'base' metals such as copper, zinc, nickel and steel (not even a portion of 'precious' metals such as gold or silver). This system allows the government to create paper and 'digital' money 'out of thin air' and funds the wars and corruption we now have (without the politically sensitive use of tax increases). The redeemability of Fed notes for gold by other nations was ended in 1971 by Pres. Nixon (because we were running out of gold), and creation of new money has soared since then ('monetary inflation' which causes 'price inflation'). As a result, the USD has lost about 90% of its value (purchasing power) for most items since 1971!

We have abused our money by excessive creation of new dollars, and many nations are selling their USD-denominated assets due to fear their holdings will lose most of their value as we crash. China and Japan are the most exposed (with about $1.3 tn each of US debt; bonds), with S. Korea next, all due to acquisition of dollars from their exports to us. The IMF and our own rating agency Standard and Poors have warned the world that the US economy and dollar are in trouble.

The **Trend** is to use less of the USD as a 'reserve currency' for international transactions. This will; 1. Reduce demand for dollars, and result in a major drop in value, and 2. Limit the USA's ability to get USD denominated loans at low rates (by selling bonds), and then repay them with newly created dollars.

Countries we buy imports from (China leads) accumulate billions of USD and buy our T-bills to get some interest (this also helps fund future purchases by the U.S.). This is a re-cycling of fake money, with interest paid by fake money, with all parties hoping it will last forever! A flight to safety is starting, and could lead to a collapse in USD value. Fake money requires demand to support its PP. Gold is safe, and this why the Russian central bank has added 570 metric tons of the metal in the past decade, and estimates are that China has added over100 tonnes since 2009! (they don't report details). Based on these gold purchases, maybe China and Russia may be planning to destroy the petrodollar system by using gold as money, and thus crash the U.S. economy by ending the USD's role as a reserve currency?

Indeed, China and Russia suggested at the Jan-2009 'World Economic Forum' in Davos that a new system is needed to replace the USD as the world's primary reserve currency, then they agreed to trade in their own currencies. In Aug-2011, China and France agreed to form a task force to discuss how the Yuan could become part of

113

the SDR (Special Drawing Rights), a basket of currencies used as money between nations. It is now 41.9% USD, 37.4% Euro, 11.3% Pound Sterling, and 9.4% Yen. It is said China wants 20% USD (was 42%), 20% Yuan, 20% Yen, 20% Euro, and 20% Pound Sterling.

In Dec-2011 China and Japan agreed to trade in their own currencies. In Jan-2012 Iran said it would sell oil to India in Rupees. China holds $1.3 trillions of USD denominated bonds and other assets, and doesn't want the USD to crash. Is this why in Feb-2013, China's central bankers suggest the world is moving "to a '1+4' system, with the greenback serving as the anchor of global payments, supplemented by 'four smaller reserve currencies' – the euro, sterling, yen and yuan." In any combination of the above trends, the USD is sliding down, and could lose over 50% of its PP! Another reason some countries, especially Russia, want to create a new financial system is to end the US ability to impose political sanctions by restricting use of the US system. Obamas early 2014 sanctions proved his concern.

The **BRICS** (Brazil, Russia, India, China, and South Africa) started trading with each other in their own currencies in 2011, thus reducing demand for the USD, and speeding its fall in value! At the July-2014 sixth summit of the BRICS in Brazil they started funding of **two multilateral financial institutions** designed to erode the dominance of the World Bank and International Monetary Fund as arbiters of the global economic system. Namely: 1) A $100 billion **New Development Bank'** (like the World Bank), and 2) a Reserve Currency Fund (like the IMF) worth another $100 billion.

China made a major announcement on Oct. 24, 2014 with the creation the **Asian Infrastructure Investment Bank (AiiBank.org)**, a multilateral development bank to provide finance to infrastructure projects in the Asia region. AIIB is regarded by some as a rival for the IMF, the World Bank and the Asian Development Bank (ADB), which are

114

dominated by developed countries like the United States. As of April 15, 2015, almost all Asian countries and most major countries outside Asia (total of 50) had joined the AIIB, except the US, Japan (which dominated the ADB) and Canada. North Korea's and Taiwan's applications for Prospective Founding Member (PFM) were rejected. The rush of our 'friends' in Europe to join is an indication of China's growing economic power. It is not clear which currency the AIIB will use. It could be the Yuan, or even the IMF SDR, with the Yuan included. Either choice would reduce the USD dominance as a reserve currency, an ominous step toward collapse of the US economy!! On Aug. 4, 2015 the IMF announced the above SDR changes would **NOT** occur at the IMF meeting to be held in Lima, Peru in Oct-2015! (see p. 116 for the results) This was pushed by the U.S. based on the fact that China's debt is 280% of their GDP, thus too weak to be part of the SDR. To gain credibility, China may announce their current holdings of gold, which have been secret since revealed as 1,054 tonnes in 2009. The changes China made in Aug-2015 to devalue the yuan by 2% (to increase exports), have added to the complexity!

Vladimir Putin, at the 11th meeting of the **Valdai International Discussion Club** in Sochi, also on Oct.24, 2014, said, *" Russia is making strides in assembling a massive new trading bloc known as the* **Eurasian Union**. *When it opens for business on January 1, 2015, Russia, Belarus, and Kazakhstan will be a barrier-free market with 170 million people and a GDP of $2.7 trillion.."* The Union will further reduce demand for the USD, and thus reduce its value (purchasing power).

China is ending many restrictions on use of its currency (the yuan, same as renminbi), and increasing its gold reserves, so it can be used in world trade and investments. The US may opt for a new currency via the IMF to pre-empt collapse of the USD, and claim (lie) that the new fiat money (Bancor?, SDR?) is a big improvement.

The IMF held its every five year meeting in Lima, Peru in Oct. 9 to11, 2015, and issued this important statement on Oct. 9; **FLASH!** On Oct. 9, the IMFs' Managing Director, Christine Lagarde, said:

"The IMF will complete an assessment of the Chinese yuan's status as a new currency for Special Drawing Rights (SDRs) before the end of 2015,

The review will determine implementation from September-2016 to allow time for central banks to adjust, including their computers. In November-2015, the IMF will decide whether to extend the current valuation of the SDR or whether to add the RMB to this basket for five years (2016-2021)." (Note; The 'RMB' is the Remnimbi, same as Yuan)

This is good news for China, but bad for the USA!! Our share of the SDR may be reduced to 20% (a drop from 41.9% !), with a corresponding decrease in our world political and economic power. This is how empires fail!

China is under pressure by the IMF to be more transparent in its financial status and deals if it wants to join the SDR. Thus China is now reporting its increase in gold holdings monthly, instead of every five years! Bloomberg reported in Oct-2015 that Chinese gold holdings went from 53.93 to 54.45 million ounces (1,694 tonnes) as of Aug-2015, marking a 1% increase for a single month. They claimed 1,054 tonnes in 2009. **A 61% increase in six years!!**

China's disclosure of gold reserves in July-2015 was met with skepticism, with many experts believing a significant portion of their reserves was omitted from official numbers. Despite being tied with India as the world's top gold consumer, China only has 1.6% of its foreign reserves in gold – a minuscule amount when compared to USA's 73% or Germanys' 67%.

China is but one of several countries, including Russia and Kazakhstan, geared towards increasing their gold reserves. The trend of most central banks amassing gold is a fairly recent one. Until just a few years ago, they had been net sellers for decades. I suggest this is a defense against possible major decline in leading fiat currencies such as the USD. The USA Fed claims to have 8,134 tonnes now (needs an audit), a major decline since its holdings of 20,297 in 1950 (up from 5,998 in 1925). The 1950 amount was due to payments received for WW2 war goods, but declined due to redemptions of paper USD notes for gold by other countries as we created massive amounts of new money to pay for 'war and welfare' after 1945. Nixon cutoff the gold losses by ending redemption in Aug-1971. We have created new money to even greater excess ever since (so have most countries) leading to 90% loss of USD purchasing power, as measured by price inflation.

To counter this growth in economic power of other nations, and the value of their currencies to make deals (leaving the USA and USD out), we must end excessive expansion of our money supply (which lowers the value –purchasing power- of the USD)!

My solution is to immediately; 1) abolish the Fed and legal .tender laws, 2) allow free-banking (no license or location limits, just full disclosure of assets and liabilities**), 3) allow private mints (all mints must hold 100% reserves for redemption of paper notes and token coins issued), 4)** make all current Fed Notes redeemable in gold by anyone on demand (and create no new notes, physical or digital), and 5) use gold in coins (such as a small disc in the center). This is the classic 'Gold Standard'. It prevents the government from creating money 'out of thin air', ends the moral hazard (doing risky deals because you expect to be bailed-out if they fail) of 'lender of last resort' to banks, makes bailouts 'unfundable', and has always resulted in more prosperity and fewer and smaller wars and business cycles. There will be no 'run' to get rid of Fed Notes because they will ALL be redeemable in gold the day the new system is announced (100% reserves in my plan). The amount of gold per current Fed Note dollars would be set by dividing the amount of gold we own (8,134 metric tonnes; subject to audit) by the number of dollars issued (M3, about $14 tn), which yields two ten-thousands of a troy ounce per dollar, or $50,000 per ounce with current 'dollars'. After the new system starts, Fed notes would be exchanged for new money denominated in weight of gold. Prices (and government taxes and fees) would also be shown in weight of gold. I predict that once the US converts to gold, all nations will, or Sellers won't accept their trash paper.

Of course, it follows that we should resign from the meddling groups such as the International Monetary Fund (IMF), World Bank, Bank of International Settlements (BIS), and the G-20, all of which only exist to patch and pamper the world's fake money system. For more detail, refer to essays in Appendix 2.

2) Taxes, Spending, and Debt: a) to g)

Note: Per USDebtClock.org, the USA is spending at the rate of $3.7 tn per year, with a budget deficit of $500 bn (which must be borrowed). Annual spending for Social Security is $883 bn, Medicare/Medicaid $968 bn, and Defense and Wars $586 bn. The national debt is $18.4 tn and Gross Domestic Product (GDP; the size of the national economy) is $17.9 tn. Thus our debt is 103% of GDP, a dangerous situation!

   a) Taxes (all levels of government; city, county, federal): As explained by 'Supply Side' economic policy (see P.C. Robert's books on P. 133), low taxes and regulation, are the first steps to renewing investor confidence and creating incentive for producers to expand their firms. This leads to new jobs and economic recovery. Our complex tax laws are often immoral, and always costly to comply with and enforce. Many taxes and deductions are part of the government's social and economic planning (which they shouldn't be involved in at all), and often do more harm than good. Again, Liberals-**Progressives reject the incentive logic of how lower taxes create jobs,** and prefer to increase taxes on 'the rich' to make them pay their 'fair share'. They purposely ignore that the top 10 percent of income earners pay about 70 percent of all federal income taxes though they earn only 43 percent of all income. Isn't that enough??

Solution: I recommend; 1) End the capital gains tax, use a flat-tax on personal income (around 15%, with no 'deductions', and reduce it as national debt is paid), and phase-out property taxes (use tuition for schools, etc.) 2). Start a Federal sales tax (around 5% would probably work; adjust as reduced government spending occurs, with no deductions (not a VAT with hidden layers), 3) Charge 'User Fees' wherever practical. This would apply to now 'free' services such as libraries, pools, and highways (more than now), 4) reduce business taxes, and 5) Convert our monetary system to my 'Private Gold Standard' (p. 153) .

..b) General Domestic Spending: The changes I suggest below will save about $800 bn per year (25% of current spending; per USDebtClock.org). We should; 1. Eliminate unconstitutional cabinet-level departments (Education, Energy, Agriculture, Homeland Security, HUD, 'Health, Education and Welfare', etc.) and just retain parts of State, Commerce, Defense, and Treasury, 2. End all programs such as National Endowment for the Arts, National Endowment for Democracy (NED; this is often used to illegally fund and organize revolutions in other countries), NPR, Peace Corps, AMTRAC, Import-Export Bank, AFDC, Food Stamps, Unemployment Pay, 3. End Pell Grants and Tuition Loans for college students and grants to professors (they flood the college industry with money and allow excessive spending and tuition increases by colleges), etc., and 4. Reduce FDA, and EPA to advisory roles, with enforcement by states. Welfare programs such as AFDC (Aid to Families with Dependent Children) actually lead to more broken families as some fathers leave when they qualify for AFDC or rent subsidies. These 'social' programs are justified as serving the 'disadvantaged' or 'underprivileged'; notice the 'victim' orientation of these terms. Conversely, Progressives view successful people with good incomes as 'privileged' or 'lucky' and say they should be forced to pay higher rates called their 'fair share', better called 'a penalty on success'! The top 10% of earners already pay about 60% of the tax dollars received by the government; isn't that enough?? Note that 'dollars paid' is what counts, not percent. All of these 'social' programs are unconstitutional, and must end. Some are desirable, but should be funded by voluntary donations (private charity). 'Privatization' of many current government functions (roads, schools, utilities, medical, pensions, transportation, etc.) is a proven way to cut costs.

c) Social Security: This cost $883 bn in FY 2015, thus 24% of spending, and growing yearly. The present system is a welfare program for seniors, paid to them by payments from current workers. There is no 'Trust Fund', just a bucket of IOUs called T-Bills issued by a broke government! Seniors have no equity (ownership) of the amounts they have paid-in to FICA in their working years (and contributions by their employers) and the government can stop paybacks (checks from the government) to seniors at any time. It is a devious plan and must be reformed before it fails (goes broke due to more recipients than payers) and hurts many people who are planning for it, or already dependent on it.

My transition plan is to; 1) Keep the present plan in force for people age 55 or older, make paybacks proportional to amounts paid in (now immigrants get nearly full pay, with a low history of pay-ins), extend start date of payback to age 70, and grant equity ownership for pay-ins already made, 2) Reduce payback amounts as needed (due to reduced program income), with five years advance notice, 3) End 'contributions' by employers, and 4) Require people age 18 to 55 to join the new plan or go 'on their own'. Either way, they will get credit/payment for their prior pay-ins, with interest.

The current program is immoral because it depends on robbing the younger generation for 'contributions' (pay-ins) sent directly to current 'recipients' of paybacks, and is unsustainable because costs are rising while 'contributors' are declining in number and income.

My proposed new program, 'Redick's Private Pension Plan', is similar to the plan in Chile since the hugely successful new version started in 1981. José Piñera, who as Chile's Minister of Labor and privatized their state pension system, is co-chairman of the Cato Institute's 'Project on Social Security Privatization'; (Cato.org). See it at; http://www.cato.org/pubs/policy_report/pr-ja-jp.html.

My Plan is optional (individuals join if they wish) where citizen contributions would be invested by private investment fund firms chosen by the citizen, and the citizen would own the account equity. Growth in value would be tax free. A government regulatory body would set some broad investment diversification rules, to avoid high-risk or politicized investments by the fund managers. The contribution amount (weekly or monthly; a percent of pretax pay, or other personal funds) would be chosen by the citizen based on his choice of retirement age. This would encourage middle-class and low income people to start an account, which they would normally view as 'only for the rich'. This program has proven very popular in Chile (90% of workers joined!) due to the ownership aspect, which fosters personal responsibility. There are many side benefits such as increasing capital available for investment (by the pension fund firms) which reduces unemployment, plus better social and economic conditions in Chile. Go to the link above for more details.

The 'private' and 'personal' aspects of my Plan will lead to more personal responsibility in our society, including more work, saving and good relations with the family and friends who will help care for the aged. Poverty cases can be served by private charity. The attitude of 'the government owes us everything' and 'it's OK to take others people's money to pay for my benefits' will fade. Thus, my plan is both moral and sustainable.

d) Medicare and Medicaid; This annual spending was $968.2 bn in FY 2015, thus 26.4% of Federal spending (and growing yearly). The changes below will save about $300 bn per year (31% of current), then lower with Medicaid funding shifted to the States. End both programs at the federal level over a five year transition period (to allow people to make changes) and replace it with my free-market plan shown in Chapter 3, item 8. This plan emphasizes use of Health Savings Accounts (HSA), owned by each person (and useable in any state, or as a bequest at death), and funded by state government, employers (at their option), and donations. The person uses the money to 'shop around' and pay doctors, clinic plans, or insurance firms directly. This has proven to reduce costs and increase personal responsibility, such as avoiding obesity, alcohol, and smoking. People are stingy with spending their HSA funds, so abuse and unneeded tests and drugs are reduced! Making all licenses optional brings patient choice and competition to the current pricing cartel held by the AMA (American Medical Association; they pay Congress well). We now have only 'Cadillac' level medical service. This plan will allow nurses (or Physician Assistants) to open their own clinics for lower-level problems, at about one-third the cost per visit! If you prefer to pay about $200 to see an M.D. for a sore thumb, fine, go to one. Some people say that others are too stupid to select non-MD services, but I say 'Mind your own business and let others manage theirs'. This attitude of excess regulation and licensing (to protect and restrict us, and limit competition; see # 26 on P. 100) is a key reason how government and health costs have gotten too big and oppressive!

e) Defense and Foreign Spending (including foreign aid, the CIA, and all US military activities and bases): This was $586 bn, thus 16% of FY 2015 Federal spending. The changes below will save about $400 bn per year (68% of current). We must; 1. End Empire-USA and our self-appointed role as the world's Policeman, Boss, and Bully, 2. End the illegal and immoral wars and occupations of Afghanistan (for access to build a pipeline to Turkmenistan, and land for bases), Iraq (for its oil, land for bases, and defense of Israel), and Libya (for oil and to expel China) in an orderly manner, not to exceed one year, 3. Offer reparations for our share of war damage and murdering of their people, 4. Close all foreign bases, and create a jobs and education program for; a) the returning troops who are discharged, and b) newly unemployed workers for domestic defense contractors, 5) resign from the UN (embassies give adequate contact with other governments; the UN is a cesspool of politics), NATO, and other mutual-defense treaties, and 6) End all 'foreign aid', most of which should be called 'bribery of foreign leaders'. In general, mind our own business, use purchase negotiations rather than war to get oil, and end special treatment of Israel and any other nation that has political favor and power in the US Congress (often due to bribes and threats to Congress persons). In accordance with the reduced missions above, we must reduce; 1. The number of military personnel and facilities, and 2. Development and production of contractor-provided military equipment and services. Medical treatment and other benefits for military veterans (not contractors) should be continued; these troopers are the victims of our warmonger politicians.

f) Debt: Both federal and personal debt have soared in recent years. Loose money stimulates spending! Federal debt is $18.4 tn, debt held by the public (mortgages, credit cards, student loans, etc.) has jumped to $16.4 tn (about equal to GDP!!), and unfunded future debt (for entitlements) is $124 tn!! (see Table 1, P. 27).

In calendar year 2015, the U.S. government will spend around $280 billion in **net** interest on its debt, according to the Congressional Budget Office — a figure that is expected to spiral ever higher in coming years. Current low interest rates are a key factor in keeping the government's interest expense burden low. If we don't reduce our deficits (less spending), the USD will lose its 'safe haven' and 'reserve currency' status (allows creation of new money to pay bills) and interest rates for borrowing will soar to unsustainable (unpayable) levels.

Of course, we must eventually pay the loan principal too! My plan for reduced spending will reduce risk for our lenders (less creation of new money, less loss of dollar value) and help prevent an increase in rates. If we don't reduce spending soon, we will have an economic crash similar to the PIIGS (Portugal, Italy, Ireland, Greece, Spain) in Europe, and no entity is big enough to bail us out!

g) Unconstitutional and Abusive Laws and Programs:

The list is too long to show here, but key ones to end are; 1) ''Signing statements' by Presidents that change the law or project involved, 2) 'Legal findings' and the Military Commissions Act of 2006 (MCA) that allow torture and detainment of suspects (terror and other) based only on an accusation by an informant or government official, 3) The Patriot Act and TSA, 4) The Williams Act of 1968 that made hostile takeovers difficult and helped incompetent and corrupt corporate officers and Directors keep their jobs and abuse their shareholders (excess pay, etc.), 5) the Exchange Stabilization Fund (ESF), created by FDR to distort the precious metals market, 6) The 'Real ID Act', 7) All minimum wage laws, 8) All laws related to the counterproductive War on Drugs (it creates more sellers-pushers and users), including Asset Forfeiture laws, 9) End Presidential power to start wars by 'Executive Order' without Congressional approval (or within 60 days of an imminent attack; part of this problem is that the cowards in Congress don't want to go on record as being for or against a war), indeed end the 'Imperial Presidency' and all of its Executive Orders - past and future-, most of which are unconstitutional or illegal, and none authorized by Congress), and 10) The Fannie Mae (stock code FNM) and Freddie Mac (FRE) 'bankers' that allowed retail banks to run amok selling bad-credit, no-doc, and liar mortgages, and then sold them to Wall Street bankers who mixed them with other debt, falsely labeled them AAA (with the help of corrupt rating firms), then 'packaged' and sold them worldwide, which was a big part of the crash of 2008!

3. 'Referendum' and 'Balanced Budget' Amendments:
a) The Swiss have been very successful in controlling government abuses and excesses by use of their referendum laws which allow then to; 1) remove legislators from office (recall), 2) pass laws that they want but can't get the self-serving legislators to pass, and 3) repeal laws that they don't like. This keeps the legislators alert to comply with the voter's wishes. I suggest a similar set of laws be invoked in the USA, and
b) A Balanced Budget amendment will give us a powerful tool to limit spending. Politicians will like it since they can claim; 'We want to give you more, but our hands are tied!'

How My Plan Will 'Restore Peace and Prosperity'

If started in early 2017 (with a new President!), the above ideas and solutions will reduce total annual spending enough to create a budget surplus by late 2020. This will allow us to start paying-down our debt, and end the threat of a declining monetary system (by then on the gold standard I hope), and economy. The alternate is to keep spending and destroy the U.S. Dollar and our economy!

Thanks for your time and interest in reading this book. As you go forth to 'Occupy Peace Now'. Fight hard, but with no violence or abuse of the personal or property rights of other people or firms. I predict we will win, just as our 1776 Founders did.

Best regards, Dave Redick

************ End of Book Text **************

Blank

Blank

Part 2: Contents: 1) Authors, Books, Sources P. 128, 2) Appendices p.136, 3) Glossary P. 147, 4) Daves' Bio P.156, 5) Index P. 157.

1) Recommended; A. Authors P. 128, B. Books P. 132, and C. Info Sources, P. 134

A. Authors (alpha order)

1. Pat Buchanan: In his book **'Day of Reckoning**: How Hubris, Ideology, and Greed Are Tearing America Apart", 2006, Pat says that America is facing a crisis from which it may not survive. He argues that the effects of mass immigration, ineffective foreign policy, an overextended military, and the worship of "free trade" are leading the country on a path of destruction. Pat has written eleven books including; 'The Unnecessary War', 'A Republic Not An Empire', 'The Death of the West', and 'Suicide of a Superpower', 2011.

2. Douglas R. Casey: In **'Crisis Investing'**, 1979, Doug predicted a major depression due to government intervention. He; 1) Is an independent thinker, with 'on the ground' business experience (not biased by academic rules and vanity), 2) Supports liberty, the gold standard, and limited government as the path to peace and prosperity, and 3) Has written eleven other books about investing and government. See his articles: 1) Feb-2012 about war, oil, and gold at: lewrockwell.com/casey/casey108, 2) Mar-2012, 'The Ascendence of Sociopaths in US Governance' lewrockwell.com/casey/casey112, and 3) Nov-2012 'The America That Was – Now the United (Police) State of America', lewrockwell.com/casey/casey139 . His archives are at; lewrockwell.com/casey/casey-arch, and caseyresearch.com/cdd/archives.

3. Stephen Greenhut is Vice President of Journalism at the Franklin Center for Government and Public Integrity (FranklinCenterhq.org). His books are. 'Plunder!, How Public Employee Unions are Raiding Treasuries...' in 2010 (see SEIU.org), and "Abuse of Power: How the Government Misuses Eminent Domain." in 2004.

4. F. A. Hayek, Nobel Laureate. See; 'Denationalisation of Money: The Argument Refined', 1976, which puts forth the case to; 1) end the government monopoly on money creation, 2) let anyone create money, and 3) let the free market determine which type of money is used.

5. Ron Holland is an international retirement consultant, public speaker, stockbroker and author of three books (including Escape the Pension Trap) and numerous articles and special reports. He is a strong proponent of global investment diversification outside U.S. markets and the dollar as protection from America's exploding national debt. See www.RonHolland.com, www.bfi-consulting.com , and as a contributor to www.thedailybell.com

6. Matt Kibbe wrote ' Hostile Takeover LP: Resisting Centralized Government's Stranglehold on America' (Jun 19, 2012). It promotes a grass-roots takeover of the Republican Party leadership, and restoration of original principles of limited gov't, comply with the Constitution, sound money, etc. **(A good complement to Dave's top-down approach!)** He is CEO of freedomworks.org , co-founded by former Rep. Dick Armey.

7. John Mackey, CEO of Whole Foods, wrote 'Conscious Capitalism: Liberating the Heroic Spirit of Business' , with Rajendra Sisodia and Bill George (Jan 15, 2013). He describes how good treatment of customers and staff (they have HSA accounts, P. 68 above) is the path to profits. He also wrote 'Be the Solution: How Entrepreneurs and Conscious Capitalists Can Solve All the Worlds Problems' with M. Strong (Mar-2009). More at ConsciousCapitalism.org

8. Eric Margolis; 'American Raj', 2008. He is an American with French and Canadian ties. His father was in the Foreign Service and he grew up in in the Mid East. As a long time foreign correspondent for the Toronto Star, and others, he has traveled the world and has great insight about world events. See http://www.ericmargolis.com/

9. **Donald W. Miller, Jr., M.D.** is a cardiac surgeon and Professor of Surgery at the University of Washington in Seattle. He is a member of Doctors for Disaster Preparedness and writes on politics, health and medicine. For a start, see his excellent 'A Fourteen Point Plan for a Post-Wilsonian America' at http://www.lewrockwell.com/orig2/miller2.html, and his archives at www.lewrockwell.com. His web site is www.donaldmiller.com, which includes his CV and bio.

10. **Gary K. North** Ph.D. (born 1942) writes on economics, history, and theology. He received a PhD in history from the University of California, Riverside in 1972, and served as research assistant for **Congressman Ron Paul in 1976** This Nov-2012 article analyzes the US economic situation; 'Government Safety Nets Are Made With Fiat Money', at http://www.garynorth.com/public/10347.cfm . His blog is garynorth.com, and news at teapartyeconomist.com

11. **Rep. Ron Paul M.D. (R, TX-14), 'The Revolution: A Manifesto',** April 2008, and **'End the Fed'** in Sep-2009, Republican candidate for President in 2008 and 2012. Dr. Paul says we have been lied to, robbed and used by our own government. Dr. Paul ended his last term as a Congressman in Jan-2013. See his archives at http://www.lewrockwell.com/paul/paul-arch.html, and his ongoing activity at CampaignforLiberty.org, and 'unofficial' news at ronpaul.com and dailypaul.com. Rep. Paul Broun (R-GA-10) says he will continue Ron's work.

p12. **James Quinn,** is Senior Director of Strategic Planning for a major university, and author of a series of essays on world financial affairs. See: 'What Happened to the American Dream', (Dec-2008) at http://www.financialsense.com/editorials/quinn/2008/1224.html , and 'The Law of Unintended Consequences: 20th Century and Beyond' (Jan-2009). For more, go to http://seekingalpha.com/author/james-quinn , www.financialsense.com/editorials/quinn/2009/0218, http://www.informationclearinghouse.info/article33527.html and his main site; http://www.theburningplatform.com/ .

13. Paul Craig Roberts, Ph.D., is an economist and author of nine books (visit Amazon.com), and many articles on economics and politics; all non-PC, based on fact and logic, and seeking the truth. Recent books are; a) 'The Neoconservative Threat..', planned for Nov-2015, b) 'How America was Lost', Mar-2014. He; 1) Holds a Ph.D. from the University of Virginia, and was a post-graduate at the University of California, Berkeley, and Oxford University where he was a member of Merton College, 2) Worked for Rep. Jack Kemp and Pres. Reagan on the implementation of 'Supply Side' economics (reduce taxes and regulation to increase incentive for investment), leading to his book 'The Supply-Side Revolution' in 1984, 3) Is Chairman of the Institute for Political Economy, and a Research Fellow at the Independent Institute, 4) Is a former; a) Associate Editor of the Wall Street Journal, b) Contributing editor for National Review, and c) Assistant Secretary of the U.S. Treasury, and 5) Is the John M. Olin Fellow at the Institute for Political Economy and a Senior Research Fellow at the Hoover Institution, Stanford University. His internet columns have attracted a worldwide following. See his site paulcraigroberts.org (click 'Articles' for archives), and his full story at en.wikipedia.org/wiki/Paul_Craig_Roberts.

14. Murray Rothbard Ph.D., A great Austrian economist, Professor, and prolific author. See 'What has the Government Done to our Money?' and more at
 http://www.mises.org/money.asp

15. **Peter Schiff** is President of Euro Pacific Capital and author of 'The Little Book of Bull Moves in Bear Markets' in 2008, 'Crash Proof: How to Profit from the Coming Economic Collapse' in 2007 (then a '2.0' version in 2011) and 'The Real Crash' in 2012. All give 'real life' ideas for economics and investing. See his business site http://www.europac.net/, and archives at http://www.lewrockwell.com/schiff/schiff-arch.html

16. Robert Wenzel is editor and publisher of the 'Economic Policy Journal' (EconomicPolicyJournal.com) which provides a steady supply of free-market analysis on a broad range of topics.

17. Thomas E. Woods, Jr. Ph.D. holds a bachelor's degree in history from Harvard and his master's, M.Phil., and Ph.D. in history from Columbia University. He is the author of eleven books, most recently *Rollback: Repealing Big Government Before the Coming Fiscal Collapse*. His other books include the *New York Times* bestsellers *Meltdown: A Free-Market Look at Why the Stock Market Collapsed,* and *Nullification: How to Resist Federal Tyranny in the 21st Century*. His website is TomWoods.com.

B. Books (in no order)

1. **'Empire of Debt'**, a 2006 book by W. Bonner and A. Wiggins. It addresses how excessive national debt and spending can drastically reduce the value of the U.S. Dollar, and cause a major depression.

2. **'The Blowback Triology'**, three books by Chalmers Johnson (Blowback-2000, Sorrows of Empire-2004, Nemesis-2007). Johnson shows how our meddling, and expensive, foreign policy does more harm than good.

3. **'The Price of Loyalty'**, 2004. by Paul O'Neill, former Sec. of Treasury. This book describes the attitudes of the Bush cabal and how they discussed plans to invade Iraq long before 9/11.

4. **'The Fall of the House of Bush'**, by Craig Unger, 2007 (also 'House of Bush, House of Saud); A journalist, he describes; 1. The true story of how the Bush cabal schemed to control the world for religion and money, and 2. The rise and collusion of the neoconservative and christian-right influences in Republican party politics

5. **'A Nation of Sheep'**, 2007, by Andrew Napolitano, (also 'Constitutional Chaos'), is about how Americans accept abuse by the government without complaint or curiosity, as long as the 'good times roll'.

6. **'Index of Economic Freedom'**, annual since 1994, The Heritage Foundation, charts economic success vs freedom; www.heritage.org/research/features/index/

7. **'The Israel Lobby'**, Mar-2006, the *London Review of Books,* an essay by John Mearsheimer and Stephen Walt, Professors at the University of Chicago, followed in 2007 by their book **'Israel Lobby and U.S. Foreign Policy'.** An analysis of the scandalous illegal and covert operations of Israel's U.S. lobby 'American-Israel Public Affairs Committee' (AIPAC) and how it impacts votes in Congress and election of Congresspersons.

8. **'The True Believer'**, by Eric Hoffer, 1951, a book which shows how people join a group or mass movement (nationalist, social, political, religious, 'Global Warming', etc.) to bring a sense of security, power, righteousness, or income to themselves.

9. **'The Great Reckoning: How the world will change in the depression of the 1990s'**, 1991, by J. Davidson and Lord R. Mogg. They warn of economic collapse of the USA due to overspending and Empire-style foreign policy.

10. Older Books that Gave Warning and Good Advice

a. 'The Law', 1850, by F. Bastiat. With his perspective of the French Revolution, he explains the fallacies of Socialism and how it must degenerate into Communism.

b. 'War is a Racket', 1935, by Smedley Butler, Maj. General, US Marines. He charges that war profiteers are behind our wars and they are all crimes.

c. 'Capitalism: The Unknown Ideal', 1967, by Ayn Rand. Discusses both the productive and moral aspects of Capitalism. Comments by Alan Greenspan (before he joined the Fed banksters in DC)

d. 'Truth and Untruth', 1972, by Rep. Paul N. 'Pete' McCloskey Jr. (R, CA-11, 1967). Pete warned us about Nixon's lies concerning Vietnam, and the broader scope of dishonesty in government. Pete was my Congressman, and I helped in his first election campaign in 1967.

e. 'A Time for Truth', 1979, by William Simon. Bill warned us of the damage being caused by excess spending, taxes, and the debasement of our currency.

f. 'An American Renaissance', 1979, by Rep. Jack Kemp. Jack sent an upbeat message on how less government spending and lower taxes would produce more growth, all based on his support of Austrian economics. His landmark '**Economic Recovery Tax Act of 1981'** (Pub.L. 97-34), also known as the **ERTA** or "**Kemp-Roth Tax Cut**," was a federal law enacted in 1981. It was an act "to amend the Internal Revenue Code of 1954 to encourage economic growth. For details go to;
http://en.wikipedia.org/wiki/Economic_Recovery_Tax_Act_of_19 81

g. 'Restoring the American Dream', 1979, by Robert Ringer. Robert warned us of a trend in the USA to expect a 'free lunch', and how we can reverse the trend with more personal responsibility and less government.

h. 'Balanced Budgets, Fiscal Responsibility and the Constitution', 1980, by R. Wagner and R. Tollison with the Cato Institute (Monograph # 1). Discusses how government 'stimulus' spending does more harm than good.

C. Info Sources on Economics and Government:

1. Articles, Consulting; TrendsReasearch.com, OccupyPeace.us, PaulCraigRoberts.org, ActivistPost.com, LewRockwell.com, Antiwar.com, FFF.org, VDare.com, Reason.org, Cato.org, PacificReasearch.org, Fee.org, pgpf.com, Independent.org, PacificLegal.org , RLC.org, Mises.org, WindRockWealth.com, AntiWar.com, TheBurningPlatform.com, EconomicPolicyJournal.com .

2. Data:
en.wikipedia.org/wiki/Money_supply, mises.org, shadowstats.com, gao.gov, MoneyWatch.com,

history.com/minisites/money/viewPage?pageId=52498,
usgovernmentspending.com, cia.gov, USDebtClock.org,
fms.treas.gov, gold.org, GATA.org, MyGovCost.org,

2. Appendices:

****** Appendix 1 ******

'Wars and the Lies That Start Them'

By David Redick

Published Mon. SEP 10, 2007   Wisconsin State Journal www.madison.com. a regional daily newspaper based in Madison, WI)

ALSO OCT.2, 2007 IN YORK NEWS TIMES, YORK, NE; http://www.yorknewstimes.com/stories/100207/editorial_warlies.s html)

And, http://www.activistpost.com/2010/12/13-lies-abbreviated-history-of-us.html#more

****

Our presidents, and their complicit henchmen, have lied us into every war since the revolution in 1776.

Their real reasons have not been legal, constitutional, or politically acceptable, so they invent one or more false reasons that they can "sell " to the people.

Sadly, most people believe the lies, and proudly support them as "wars for defense. " They can 't imagine that our leaders would be so evil as to spend the lives of our troops to gain their hidden political and economic goals for Empire-USA.

The secret plan of Bush and his gang was to: 1) Take over all oil in the Greater Middle East (from the northern 'xxstans' to north Africa) so we don 't have to share it with China and India, 2) Land for bases, and 3) Defend Israel at any cost. Control of oil was the hidden reason for the Balkans, Afghan, Libya, and Iraq (Mali?) invasions and occupations.

Iran and Syria are the next targets.

The war drums are beating in Washington to justify bombing Iran, so this is a good time to consider whether our leaders are lying again. Here are the facts on how we got into a few major wars. Each one could be a book, so please forgive the brevity.

War of 1812

Lies: In 1812, Congress declared war on England based primarily on their kidnapping ("impressment") of our sailors at sea. **Truth:** To drive England out of North America and get southern land. The war started with our invasion of Canada, at Detroit. We burned their Parliament buildings in York (now Toronto), so they burned DC ! The 'Star Spangled Banner' was written a week later when British boats shelled Baltimore Harbor.

Mexican-American War

Lies: Fight to defend our Texas border with Mexico. **Truth**: We invaded to expand, and took the northern half of Mexico, now our entire Southwest region (to Sonoma, CA).

Civil War

Lies: Fight to end slavery and preserve the union. **Truth**: The South seceded due to economic abuse by the North. It was an invasion by the North, not a civil war! The Emancipation Dec. ended slavery only in Southern states.

Spanish-American War

Lies: Spain blew-up the U.S. battleship Maine in Cuba's Havana harbor. **Truth:** The accidental explosion was used to invade Cuba, steal Puerto Rico, annex Hawaii, and kill 200,000 locals to put a base in the Philippines.

World War I

Lies: Join Europe to "Make the World Safe for Democracy " **Truth:** Wilson was convinced to join by U.S. war-goods firms who wanted the U.S. to be one of the peace negotiators so they would be paid by England and France. Thus, thousands of our troops died, and brought home the flu epidemic of 1918 that killed millions in the U.S.!

World War II

Lies: Defend the United States from unprovoked attacks by Japan. **Truth**: FDR wanted to prevent Germany from becoming a world power, so he poked Japan until he got an "incident."

Korean War

Lies: Defend America. **Truth:** Truman and the generals wanted a reason to have troops in the Far East area of our Empire.

Vietnam War

Lies: Johnson said Vietnam attacked our ships in the Gulf of Tonkin. **Truth:** The United States (and the Rockefellers) didn't want to lose the southeast Asia region, and its oil, to China.

Gulf War

Lies: To defend Kuwait from Iraq. **Truth:** Saddam was a threat to Israel, and we wanted his oil.

Balkans

Lies: Prevent Serb killing of Bosnians. **Truth:** Get the Chinese out of Eastern Europe and Caspian Sea areas so they couldn't get control of the oil.

Afghanistan

Lies: The Taliban were hiding Osama. **Truth:** To build a gas/oil pipeline from the northern Turkmenistan to a warm water port near Karachi.

Iraq Invasion

Lies: Stop use of WMDs, or bring democracy. **Truth:** Oil, defense of Israel, land for permanent bases and restore oil sales in the U. S. Dollar.

Possible Iran War

Lies: They almost have an atom bomb. **Truth:** Oil for the U.S., cut off oil to China, and defense of Israel.

Syria *

Lies; Pres. Assad gassed his people, and is a threat to Israel. **Truth:** They are friendly with Russia (allows use of their Tartus sea port) and could block a pipeline from Qatar to Turkey

We must fight the Bush and Obama* gangs to stop their plans for war against Iran.

(* Oct-2015 Update)

******* **Appendix 2** *******

Dave's Published Essays:

To save typing, just click on links at Part 8 in the left margin of my site Forward-USA.org; the whole list below is there, plus updates and additions.

'1. Government Structure and Conduct

a) 'The Phases of Empires' , Aug-2010 ;   How empires rise and fall, and how five key characteristics vary for each

Phase. http://www.activistpost.com/2010/08/phases-of-empire.html#more (same as Chapter 2 herein)

http://theburningplatform.com/blog/tag/dave-redick/

http://lewrockwell.com/orig12/redick1.1.1.html 20Dec2011

  b) 'The Cost of Building and Operating Empire-USA',
  Aug-2010

How owning colonies/territories, or controlling other countries, damages the economics, civil rights, and morals of the Homeland.
 http://www.activistpost.com/2010/08/cost-of-building-and-operating-empire.html#more

  c) 'How Governments Abuse Our Patriotism'   Aug-2010

How governments promote 'Patriotism' and take advantage of it for their wars, and other abuses.
http://www.activistpost.com/2010/08/how-governments-abuse-our-patriotism.html   Aug-2010

  d) '13 Lies: An Abbreviated History of U.S. Presidents Leading Us to War'   Dec-2010

'Also named; 'Wars and the Lies that Start Them'.
Discloses how all major US wars since the Revolution were started with Lies by Presidents.
http://www.activistpost.com/2010/12/13-lies-abbreviated-history-of-us.html#more. Shown above as Appendix 1.

  e) 'The Role of 9-11 in Middle East Resource Control'
Jan-2011 ; How 9/11 was a pre-planned 'trigger' to justify the WOT and the invasions of Afghan and Iraq
http://www.activistpost.com/2011/01/role-of-9-11-in-middle-east-resource.html

f) 'Save the USA by Restoring Government to its proper Role'   Nov. 2, 2012 update of original April 22, 2011

USA governments at all levels have grown in power since our founding, and are causing great social and economic harm with their regulations, spending, and abuses. The USA is at a tipping point where spending reductions and legal reforms must be made or we will have a more severe economic crash than we have experienced since 2008. Included in Chapter 4 above.
http://www.activistpost.com/2011/04/save-usa-by-restoring-government-to-its.html#more

g) **Restoration of States Rights and Sound Money are Needed to End Decline of the USA Economy'**
Sep. 9, 2015
http://www.activistpost.com/2015/09/restoration-of-states-rights-and-sound-money-are-needed-to-end-decline-of-the-usa-economy.html
Since the Constitution was ratified in 1789, the Federal government has gained excessive power over the people, States, and monetary system. The result is less liberty, massive debt, and wars for Empire-USA. In order to reduce spending, and debt, and end wars for empire, we must return the original power to the states and people before our economy crashes!

2. Monetary Systems

a)   'Why Use Gold as Money?'   Dec-2010

The benefits of using a commodity as money, and why the market prefers gold
http://www.activistpost.com/2010/12/why-use-gold-as-money.html

b)   'How to Abolish the Fed and Convert to Gold as Money'   Jan-2011

A six-step plan to convert the US to gold as money, allow private mints, and the benefits it would bring. http://www.activistpost.com/2011/01/how-to-abolish-fed-and-convert-to-gold.html#

 c) 'The Impact of Fiat Money as the World's Reserve Currency'   Aug-2010

There is always a major currency that; 1. banks worldwide use as their reserves, and 2. is used for trade between countries, which since 1920 it has been primarily the US Dollar. After abrogating the Dollar's gold backing in 1971, the US started creating trillions of fiat paper notes - - monetary inflation - - to pay for its excessive imports (causing 'offshoring' of jobs), wars and other excesses. This excess money creation can only be done by the issuer of the world's primary reserve currency. http://www.activistpost.com/2010/09/impact-of-fiat-money-as-worlds-reserve.html#more

d) 'A Plan to Save the Euro with Gold'   Nov. 30, 2011

European 'leaders' are in a panic to save the Euro! I offer a plan that could be invoked by Euro issuing nations with no risk to current Euro owners because all existing Euro currency would immediately be backed by gold, so there would be no 'run' to dump them. http://www.activistpost.com/2011/11/three-step-plan-to-save-euro-with-gold.html#more

 e) 'Convert the USA Monetary System to Gold'   Jan. 25, 2012
This essay shows a detailed plan to implement conversion from fake Fed Notes (FFN !) to 'gold-as-money' (all free market, with private mints, no Fed, redeemable paper notes, gold weight as the unit of account, etc.) and all the positive changes that go with it.

http://www.activistpost.com/2012/01/convert-usa-monetary-system-to-gold.html#more

f) 'Germany Should Quit the Euro and Use Gold As Money', Sep. 1, 2012

The fiat Euro (no gold 'backing') gave politicians and banks a way to create new money to feed excess spending and debt. A further weakness was the hope (assumption?) that the larger nations (Germany and France) would bail out the sick nations and banks. This is like giving more heroin to an addict. **http://www.activistpost.com/2012/09/germany-should-quit-euro-and-use-gold.html#more**

g) 'Will Basel III Allow Gold Money to Prevent a Crash of the USA Economy?', Nov. 2, 2012
By upgrading gold reserves at central banks to a Tier 1 asset (same as cash) the BIS gives new respect for 'gold as money', which is a golden opportunity (nice pun!) for the USA to return to the gold standard to save its monetary system from collapse!
http://www.activistpost.com/2012/11/will-basel-iii-allow-gold-money-to.html

3. General Economic and Social Issues

a) 'How is Independent Thinking is Connected to Freedom and Prosperity'   Aug-2010 ; Explores the concept of Independent Thinking, where a person decides what to believe and do, rather than seeking the comfort of following the
mainstream. http://www.activistpost.com/2010/08/how-is-independent-thinking-connected.html

b) ' How Excess Spending, Taxation, and Controls are Destroying the US Economy' Jan-2011; How excess spending, taxation, and controls by government for wars, welfare, entitlements, subsidies, etc., mostly financed by debt or fake money from our central bank, is wrecking our economy and morals.

http://www.activistpost.com/2011/01/how-excess-spending-taxation-and.html

c) 'How Free-Market Choices Can Solve Our Health Care Problems'   March 3, 2011 ; A plan to improve care and reduce costs by; a) getting the federal government out of health care funding and control, b) end the AMA pricing cartel, and c) bringing free-market competition and choice to health care. http://www.activistpost.com/2011/03/how-free-market-choices-can-solve-our.html

e) 'Should Government Manage the Economy?' , March 15, 2011 ; The biggest divides in thinking as to the proper role of government are whether it should; 1. Manage the economy and monetary system, and be paternalistic in providing cheap or free social services, or 2. Just protect the rights of its citizens.

http://www.activistpost.com/2011/03/should-government-manage-economy.html#more

Blank

(Blank)

3. Glossary:

1. Appreciation: An increase in value, such as increased purchasing power of money. Opposite of 'depreciation'.

2. Central Bank: Whether private or owned by the government, a central bank usually has certain government-bestowed duties and privileges such as; a) The sole right to issue currency and market government securities, b) Allowed to operate in almost total secrecy to supposedly avoid political influence, c) Set interest rates, d) Buy government securities to fund government expenses, e) Stabilize the value of the currency and keep unemployment low (these may be fake duties, but sound good!), f) Serves as the 'Lender of Last Resort' to banks short of cash (a sweet deal for casino bankers!), and g) other acts. The CB managers typically work closely with their government leaders (thus politicized), and key managers may be appointed by the government. In the U.S., it is the Federal Reserve System.

3. COMEX: Formerly **'The Commodity Exchange, Inc.'**, is now a metals exchange in the CME Group (cmegroup.com), which also owns 'The New York Mercantile Exchange' (NYMEX). The other two designated contract markets in the CME Group are the Chicago Mercantile Exchange (CME) and the Chicago Board of Trade (CBOT). COMEX is a primary market for trading metals such as gold, silver, copper and aluminum. Combined with NYMEX, they are the world's largest physical metals futures trading exchange.

4. Commodities: For 'goods' (not 'services'), a commodity is substance that can be described as a standard (type, grade, etc.) and thus be considered the same substance in any market. Location doesn't matter, except for delivery cost. Generally, these are basic resources and agricultural products such as iron ore, crude oil, coal, salt, sugar, tea, coffee beans, soybeans, tobacco, aluminum, copper, rice, wheat, and precious metals. Soft commodities are goods that are grown, while hard commodities are the ones that are extracted through mining. Well-established physical commodities have actively traded spot and derivative markets. Some commodities have been used as money (in order of value and popularity; gold, silver, copper, nickel, zinc, steel).

5. Contrarian Investor; One who profits by investing against the conventional wisdom. Opposite of the Lemmings or Sheep, that prefer to be viewed as 'normal and safe' and follow the crowd despite warning signs.

6. Deflation: The opposite of Monetary Inflation; a reduction in the money supply as a % of GDP, and an increase in purchasing power of each money unit, thus lower prices. Not to be confused with 'depression' or 'depreciation'.

7. Depression: Any economic downturn where real GDP (Gross Domestic product) declines by more than 10 percent. Also; Two or more quarters of reduced GDP. A **recession** is an economic downturn that is less severe.

8. Economics: (Types, alpha order)

a. 'Austrian School' of economic thought (Hayek, von Mises, Rothbard), emphasizes the spontaneous organizing power of free market pricing, decisions by individuals, gold as money, and little or no government management or stimulation of the economy.
b. Capitalism - An 'economic system' based on private ownership, free enterprise, and minimal regulation. It offers more than economic results. **It is a moral system** that depends on willing buyers and sellers within the rule of law, not coercion and control by others. It has been re-defined as a mean, self-centered, you're on your own, 'social system' by those who prefer Socialism (sharing by force, causing a more equal but lower standard of living for all). **The U.S. now has 'Crony Capitalism'**, a damaging distortion where firms get favors from government (often in exchange for campaign donations!). It creates privilege for the few at the expense of the many.
c. Communism: The government owns all housing, agriculture, industry and transportation (almost everything but the clothes on your back). The government tells you where to live, go to college (if any), and where to work.
d. Fascism allows private ownership of businesses, but there is extensive government control and preeminence.

e. 'Keynesian Theory' (started by J. M. Keynes and now used by Krugman, Samuelson, Stiglitz, Bernanke, Reich, and Yellen) depends on massive use of government fiscal (spending) and monetary (interest rates, money supply) policy trying to create prosperity or avoid and end depressions. History and logic show the Keynes approach is unsustainable and never works for more than a year or two (longer if supported by natural resources; oil, timber, mining, etc.).

f. Monetarism: An approach identified with the 'Chicago School of economics led by Prof. Milton Friedman Ph.D. of the University of Chicago. It emphasizes management of the money supply by the Fed to control inflation and GDP growth. Most Monetarists dislike the gold standard as 'too inflexible' in changing the money supply, except by mining more gold or silver. They are wrong because they ignore how the purchasing power of gold increases with more demand. Thus, there is always 'enough'.

g. Socialism: Most of the means of production and trade (factories, railroads, etc) are owned by the government, which sets pricing, product types, etc. The government controls most wages, with an emphasis on 'fairness', need, and 'hours worked', rather than value of the service performed. High, and steeply progressive, taxes support a 'single-payer health system and pension plan

h. 'Supply Side' economics: This school of thought emphasizes incentive to invest by reductions in; **a.** capital gains and income taxes, and **b**. regulation. These should be the first steps to revive a troubled economy because they have the lasting effect of stimulating action by producers and investors. "Supply Side' was originated by economists P. C. Roberts Ph.D., Robert Mundell Ph.D., and Arthur Laffer Ph.D., and politicians Pres. Ronald Reagan and Rep. Jack Kemp in the 1980s.

9. Fiat Money: Fiat ('by decree') money is worth whatever the government says it is (face value), although the material of which it is made may have more or less market value (examples; one ounce silver dollars and worthless paper, both declared worth $1; one ounce American Eagle gold coin with face value of $50).

10. Fiscal Policy: Management of government spending to fulfill obligations, and in some cases to 'stimulate', or 'guide', the economy.

11. Free Market: A market that is free from government intervention (i.e., regulation, subsidies, price controls, or governmental monopolies, etc.). In a free market, property rights (ownership of goods and services) are voluntarily exchanged at a price and terms arranged solely by the mutual consent of sellers and buyers/consumers, with no government control of pricing, creation of new firms, pay and benefits, hiring and firing, etc.

12. Gang Theft: This occurs when one group of people in some manner overpowers another group, and forcibly takes assets from them. Most people agree that it is immoral, and should be illegal, but oddly, most people believe it is OK to employ gang-theft-by-vote to tax, restrict, or control others (usually 'the rich'), via government power as the larger group sees fit. They justify it by making their victims pay their 'fair share', or 'they got rich by luck', etc. **This in fact describes an immoral government and a 'penalty on success',** thus a reverse incentive.

13. Gross Domestic Product (GDP): The market value of all final goods and services made within the borders of a country in a year. **Gross National Product (GNP)** is GDP plus income received from other countries (interest and dividends), less similar payments made to other countries.

14. IMF: The **International Monetary Fund** is an international organization **headquartered** in Washington, DC, of "188 countries working to foster global monetary cooperation, secure financial stability, facilitate international trade, promote high employment and sustainable economic growth, and reduce poverty around the world". It was formed in 1944 as part of the Bretton Woods Agreement. (see SDR, #22 below), as was the World Bank. (#26).

15. Inflation: a. Monetary Inflation: A rapid and excessive expansion of the money supply (such as over 5% per year; more than growth of GNP); purchasing power of a given monetary unit (Dollar, etc.) is reduced, **b. Price Inflation:** Increase in current prices due to reduced purchasing power of the money caused by

150

an excessive increase in the money supply (or other factors such as reduced supply, increased demand, cartel pricing, etc.). 'Nominal' is the listed price. 'Real' is a past or future nominal price adjusted for price inflation. 'Hyper' inflation is a rapid and continuing increase of prices (over 50 %/mo.), the supply of money, and the cost of goods.

16. Internationalize: This is the process done by investors who are concerned about decline of their domestic currency values, and increased taxes, capital controls, and confiscation. At a minimum, they convert their assets to denomination in a stronger foreign currency in an 'investor friendly' country, but this does not help minimize U.S. taxes, etc. A more complete approach is to work with a professional (lawyer, accountant, Wealth Management Financial Advisor) to set up an International Business Company (or Limited Liability Corporation), a tax minimization trust, and banking, in one or more foreign jurisdictions (nations).

17. Mercantilism: An economic system where the ruling government seeks wealth, especially gold or silver bullion, by playing a protectionist role in the economy, and by encouraging exports and discouraging imports, notably through the use of import tariffs, subsidies to domestic firms, and money valuation. The opposite is a policy of laissez-faire, which says that all trade is good and that such controls are counterproductive, and usually evolve to be used as political favors.

18. Monetary Policy: Management of the monetary system; money supply, bank reserves, interest rates, etc.

19. Money: (mostly from wikipedia.org) Money is anything that is generally accepted as payment for goods and services and repayment of debts. The main functions of money are distinguished as a: medium of exchange, unit of account, and store and measure of value.

Money originated as **commodity money,** then evolved to easier-to-transport, avoid wear, 'representative' money in which a paper certificate, or base-metal coin can be redeemed by the Bearer on demand to the Issuer (Mint). However, nearly all contemporary money systems at the national level are fiat money systems. **Fiat**

money is without value as a physical commodity, and derives its value by being declared by a government to be **legal tender**; that is, it must be accepted when offered, and at certain face value (USD, Euro, etc.).

20. Principle: An underlying guide to thinking and action. A comprehensive and fundamental law, doctrine, or assumption. A rule or code of conduct.

21. Reserves: 1. Fractional Reserve Banking means the bank need only retain a certain percent of deposits on hand (typically about ten percent) and can loan the rest. In fact, this means banks can loan ten times the amount of their deposits, thereby creating new money! For example, a $1,000 deposit can be the reserve for $10,000 of new loans. **2. 'Reserve Currency'** is the money of a certain nation that by agreement or common usage; 1. can be used by banks as their 'reserve' ('good as gold') which underpins their loans and obligations, and 2. is acceptable for payments between other countries worldwide.

22. Special Drawing Rights (SDR; also see IMF): Special drawing rights (XDR or SDR) are supplementary foreign exchange reserve assets defined and maintained by the International Monetary Fund (IMF;). Their value is based on a basket of key international currencies reviewed by IMF every five years. Based on the latest review conducted on December 30, 2010, the SDR basket consists of the following four currencies: U.S. dollars ($) 41.9 % , euro (€) 37.4 %, pounds sterling (£) 11.3 %, and the Japanese yen (¥) 9.4 %.The weights assigned to each currency in the SDR basket are adjusted to take into account their current prominence in terms of international trade and national foreign exchange reserves. The most recent IMF meeting was in Oct-2015. China has expressed interest in being part of the SDR, with the USD content reduced.

The SDR is not a currency per se. They instead represent a claim to currency held by IMF member countries for which they may be exchanged. As they can only be exchanged for U.S. dollars ($), euro (€), pounds sterling (£), or Japanese yen (¥), XDRs may actually represent a potential claim on IMF member countries' non-gold foreign exchange reserves, which are usually held in those currencies. Being the unit of account for the IMF has long been the main function of the XDR.[5]

Special Drawing Rights are denoted with the ISO 4217 currency code XDR. SDRs are allocated to countries by the IMF. Private parties do not hold or use them.

(https://en.wikipedia.org/wiki/Special_drawing_rights)

23. Standards for 'Gold-as-Money' Monetary Systems
The gold standard is a monetary system in which the unit of account is weight of gold. Prices are by weight and purity.

1) The **Gold Specie Standard** is the system in which the monetary unit is associated with a circulating gold coin. (for paper notes, if any, the issuer must have 100% reserves for redeemption)

2) The **Gold Exchange Standard** may involve only the circulation of silver coins, or coins made of other metals, but the authorities will have guaranteed a fixed exchange rate with another country that is on the gold standard, hence creating a *de facto* gold standard. An example is the Bretton Woods Agreement of 1944.

3) The **Gold Bullion Standard** is a system in which gold coins do not actually circulate, but in which the authorities have agreed to sell gold bullion on demand at a fixed price.

(from http://en.wikipedia.org/wiki/Gold_standard)

4) The **Private Gold Standard;** Under this plan, money is produced by private firms in the free market where customers (users of money) decide which type and source of money they prefer, and mints compete for customers. There is no central

bank (our Fed), and government mints (run by the Treasury), if any, are optional, and have no control or privilege over the private mints.

The free market is allowed to work! The 'unit of account', and thus pricing, is **weight** of the commodity (typically gold and silver) used as money. The gold may be alloyed for hardness, etc., but only the amount of pure 24 carat gold counts. Paper notes can be used for convenience, but are only claim checks the issuer (mint) must redeem for gold by any bearer on demand.

24. SWIFT: The '**Society for Worldwide Interbank Financial Telecommunication'** (**SWIFT**) provides a network that enables financial institutions worldwide **to send and receive information** about financial transactions (but not 'execute' them) in a secure, standardized and reliable environment. The majority of international interbank messages use the SWIFT network. As of September 2010, SWIFT linked more than 9,000 financial institutions in 209 countries and territories. SWIFT is a cooperative society under Belgian law owned by its member financial institutions with offices around the world. The USA has major influence over its services

25. US Dollar Index (USDX): It is a measure of the value of the United States dollar relative to a basket of foreign currencies. It is a **weighted geometric mean** of the dollar's value compared with "basket" of 6 other major currencies which are, '% by weight': Euro (EUR), 57.6%, Japanese yen (JPY) 13.6%, Pound sterling (GBP), 11.9%, Canadian dollar (CAD), 9.1%, Swedish krona (SEK), 4.2%, and Swiss franc (CHF) 3.6% .

More at; http://en.wikipedia.org/wiki/U.S._Dollar_Index)

26. World Bank: The **World Bank** was formed in 1944 as part of the Bretton Woods Agreement. It is an international financial institution that provides loans to developing countries for capital programs. It comprises two institutions: the International Bank for Reconstruction and Development (IBRD) and the International Development Association (IDA). The World Bank is a component of the **World Bank**

154

Group, and a member of the United Nations Development Group. The World Bank's official goal is the reduction of poverty. According to its Articles of Agreement, all its decisions must be guided by a commitment to the promotion of foreign investment and international trade and to the facilitation of capital investment (see IMF, 14 above)

(Blank)

4. Biography of Dave Redick

Personal: Dave grew up with his two brothers in a middle class family near Detroit, MI. When he was 14, the family moved to an 80-acre general farm near Ann Arbor, Michigan. He has an honorable discharge from the U.S. Army Reserve.

Education and Business: Dave won a four-year tuition scholarship to the University of Michigan, based on grades, activities (Sr. Class President, sports), and need, and started in the fall of 1953. He completed his engineering degree in Feb., 1958. Upon graduation he worked as an aerospace engineer for 5 years (rocket engines and satellites) in California, then started his career in telecom sales and management. In 1965 he earned an MBA in Economics from Santa Clara University in Santa Clara, CA, and after management positions in several other firms, in 1995 became VP Sales, then President, of a wireless engineering consulting firm www.hntelecom.com (closed, see Google). He left in 2000 to be VP and cofounder of a Silicon Valley telecom startup 'Fiberstreet' (closed, see Google), and helped raise $6 million of venture capital. In 2005 he started 'Sustainable Energy Earth', an energy consulting firm.

Political: In 1978, Dave became concerned about economic and social damage caused by counterproductive government 'management' (intervention?). He then read about and discussed this subject widely and became an activist for more cost-effective, and less abusive, government. He ran for Congress as a Libertarian in 1982 in District CA-1, then returned to his Republican roots and ran in CA-1 again in 1984 with Reagan,, and received a support letter from him. During the G. W. Bush administration, Dave became concerned about the Republican Party's departure from its core principles. In 2007 he was the Wisconsin contact for The Republican Liberty Caucus (see www.WI.RLC.org and www.RLC.org), which promotes the principles of limited government and free enterprise. In 2008 Dave founded the 'Forward USA Foundation' to promote better (usually less) government.
The website is www.Forward-USA.org.

5. Index: Page numbers are in bold if their topic is in a title or the Glossary

www.ingramcontent.com/pod-product-compliance
Lightning Source LLC
Chambersburg PA
CBHW062007280526
45787CB00005B/2002

* 9 7 8 1 5 1 7 5 5 6 6 7 9 *